Home Buyer's Guide

EVERYDAY HANDBOOKS

Home Buyer's Guide

Jack Wren

 BARNES & NOBLE, INC., NEW YORK
Publishers • Booksellers • Since 1873

Printed in the United States of America

Contents

PART III SELLING YOUR HOME

Illustrations

vii

Tables

Tables

Acknowledgments

The author is grateful to the following companies, organizations, and institutions for their assistance in providing information and illustrations.

Andersen Corporation
The Celotex Corporation
Chrysler Corporation, Airtemp Division
City Planning Commission, City of New York
Con Edison of New York
Federal Housing Administration
Federal Trade Commission
General Electric
House & Home
Interstate Commerce Commission
Jim Walter Corporation
Johns-Mansville
Kidde & Co., Inc.
Master Plan Service, Inc.
National Better Business Bureau
National Electrical Manufacturers Association
National Fire Protection Association
National Forest Products Association
Pyrotronics, Inc.
The Surety Association of America
U.S. Department of Agriculture, Forest Service
United States Gypsum
Veterans Administration
Westinghouse Electric Corporation

Introduction

Buying a house is the greatest lifetime investment made by the average family. More than half of all American families now live in their own homes. Many others living in apartments or other rental units look forward hopefully to the day they too can buy their own homes.

Home ownership can be a boon or a bane, depending upon the care and good judgment shown *before* buying. The one indispensable requisite for any type of house is sound construction. An understanding of the factors involved in selecting a house will assure maximum value for the dollars spent in purchasing it. A swarm of problems—in fact, financial nightmares—threaten the uninformed buyer.

According to Arthur Tauscher, a civil engineer specializing in home inspection, an examination of a thousand houses ten years old or more revealed that 840 were inadequately wired for current needs; 540 showed evidence of termite infestation or damage; defective plumbing, including corroded pipes or insufficient water pressure, was discovered in 180 homes; 160 structures were in need of a new heating unit; 45 had water seepage in the basement; and 30 houses were structurally deficient.

All these problems could have been avoided if, when buying their homes, the prospective purchasers had adhered to the ancient Latin maxim *caveat emptor*—let the buyer beware.

This book, based on information obtained from United States Government and municipal agencies, construction experts, real estate brokers, lawyers, business and industrial concerns, and innumerable home owners, will help you avoid the costly mistakes so common in property transactions. It will provide you with facts about sound house construction, building codes and zoning regulations, agreements with contractors, mortgages, financing, taxes and exemptions, special assessments, and how to sell your house.

ADVANTAGES OF OWNING YOUR HOME

Space and privacy are the two major conveniences you will acquire when you purchase a home. More space within a house affords both the privacy and the freedom of movement that are not possible in the average apartment. There is room for a variety of household appliances, including laundry equipment. A private garage or parking site is always available. Even in urban areas, a house has some open space that can be used for outdoor living, a distinct advantage during the warm months.

Houses can be changed to meet new family living patterns by rearranging interiors, making alterations, or expanding. It is not necessary to uproot the family by moving to a new location in order to acquire additional living space. There is also an opportunity to express individuality, inside and out, through personal touches that make each house distinctive from its neighbors.

One-family residential communities are free of much traffic, noise, and dirt that are common in densely populated urban areas. Home owners usually are more considerate of their neighbors' right to quiet enjoyment of their property. Furthermore, there is a feeling of identity with the neighborhood and an opportunity to be more directly in control of your environment through participation in community activities.

The home buyer acquires not only more indoor and outdoor living space, but also a sound investment. A portion of the monthly mortgage payment represents compulsory savings that steadily augment the amount of this investment until the property is debt free. Utilizing the business technique of leverage, the home owner uses the lender's money to own his house outright eventually. During inflationary periods, the borrower pays off his debt with money of declining value. At the same time, inflation usually increases the property's value. Prices of commodities, including real property, rise while money loses its former buying power. Aside from being more expensive than most commodities, the market price of houses also increases because people will pay more for a house. Rents on apartments, too, increase during inflationary spirals, but the home owner acquires equity in his property rather than rent receipts.

As compared to apartment rental, home ownership entails certain tax advantages. Income tax deductions are permitted on real estate taxes and mortgage interest. If the property produces an income through rental of an apartment, as in a two-family house or a garage rental, the owner is entitled to a tax deduction for expenses apportioned according to the space used. The home owner is also provided with a cushion against uninsured casualty losses, such as hurricane, windstorm, fire, flood, and similar causes; these losses, too, are tax deductible.

Trees, shrubs, flowers, and green lawns are distinctive features which characterize the amenable environment of suburbia. More outdoor living space contributes to felicity of home and affords safer play areas for children.

DISADVANTAGES OF OWNING YOUR HOME

Before buying your home, you should also consider the disadvantages. The large down payment for a house deprives the purchaser of the use and interest on this sum. This may entail a hardship for those who require ready cash for business investment or college expenses. All dwellings require continuing expenditures for maintenance, taxes, insurance, fuel, and commutation. To those who prefer proximity to their employment or business in the city, commuting may be both expensive and exhausting. Garden maintenance costs must be added by those who do not enjoy doing chores of this type themselves.

Part I

Choosing Your Home

Chapter 1

Family Requirements, Present and Future

Americans are among the most mobile people in the world; relatively few families spend their lifetimes in the same house. Family-life patterns indicate that about every five years the dwelling needs of the average family change.

From one to five years after marriage, living needs usually do not extend beyond one room with kitchenette and bath, or a one-bedroom apartment.

In the next five to ten years, one or two children have been added to the family, and two or three bedrooms and more storage areas are needed.

Within ten to fifteen years after marriage, the average family has three children and requires a larger living unit, perhaps with a second bath.

In the next ten years, as the children mature, there is no basic change regarding space. Any residential change is likely to be dictated by the husband's employment transfer to another city, or a desire to locate in a better or different neighborhood.

From twenty-five to forty years after marriage, the grown children either go to college or marry. During this period space needs diminish correspondingly.

After forty years, the "family" is often reduced to one person whose space needs are no greater than those of a newly married couple.

Most prospective house buyers desire more space than they can easily afford. The soundest approach is to establish your own method of priorities. List the rooms your family requires for its activities, then limit the size of these space units.

While planning, consider the dwelling's resale value. A house which contains the basic conveniences and comforts for your family will usually be suitable for the next family as well.

Although a structure's exterior is important, primary attention should be given to the interior. A convenient kitchen or a half-bath, sometimes called a powder room, is more essential than carved cornices or an unused attic.

Maturing children require an expanding house. Carefully planning dual purpose rooms, such as allowing a family room to serve as a guest room or extra bedroom, will increase a home's utilitarian and monetary value. All well-planned interiors follow pleasantly defined patterns. Careful attention to comfortably proportioned rooms, family traffic through them, the location of windows and doors, soft but clear lighting, sufficient floor area and storage space will contribute to the harmony of family life.

Recreational, medical, educational, and cultural requirements vary with a family's changing living patterns. List the factors you consider essential to your family's activities now and in the future. Determining how much travel time you and members of your family are willing to spend to reach the needed facilities will help you select the right location for your home. For example, if you enjoy golf, you will prefer a locality that has a country club or public golf course nearby. If you and your family are interested in water sports, this will be an important factor in choosing location.

Seek the house and location that will fill most of your needs. Evaluating your requirements will help you to make a selection that is best suited to your own family's living pattern.

Chapter 2

Location

CITY OR SUBURB?

Settlement patterns have always been determined by physical land features plus the type and location of natural resources. Towns and villages took root around harbors and rivers and along transportation routes which were defined by the course of rivers and mountain ranges. Later on, settlements followed railroads. Today they move in the wake of highways.

Industrial complexes are generally tied to areas by natural re-sources—supply of raw materials, water and power—and markets. However, technological advances resulting in improved transporta-tion and communication now permit greater site flexibility. Industry forms the core of urban development around which commercial enterprises, manpower, and markets exist.

Among the more stable factors near this urban nucleus are the universities, medical and cultural centers, and government facilities. Generally located on large tracts of land, these centers do not readily shift to new localities.

The automobile is still opening new regions of development away from the old transportation corridors. Nevertheless, urban growth patterns remain relatively fixed. Although cities survive changes in their immediate surroundings and in those of the region, they are in a constant state of flux. Urban sections deteriorate, and buildings and sites become obsolescent. New growth burgeons around large blighted areas, but small pockets of decay are absorbed and eliminated. Urban changes usually lag far behind economic and social needs.

Population experts predict that there will be 250 million Americans by 1980. At the turn of the twenty-first century, the country will have well over 300 million people. Without thoughtful planning to equalize population distribution, 60 million Americans will be thinly spread over 91 percent of the land while well over 240 million will be concentrated in only 9 percent of the nation.

The postwar boom followed old patterns of development and brought with it such new problems as water shortages, lack of power, and water and air pollution. Communities became aware of open space values, not only for the health and welfare of their residents, but as an indispensable condition to maintaining or increasing property values.

Beginning in the immediate postwar years, families reacted to mounting urban problems in a predictable manner by moving to the suburbs. But poor planning in outlying sections confronted the inhabitants with new problems. Undeveloped suburban areas began to vanish at the staggering rate of one million acres every year. Soaring land prices reflect the scarcity of open land encircling cities. A lot, usually 10 percent of the price of a house in the early 1950s, represented up to one-third of the total cost by the late 1960s. Within urban areas, the rising demand for existing parcels escalates prices and produces greater density (the number of people per square mile of area).

Concomitant problems in mushrooming residential suburbs, often called the bedrooms or dormitories of cities, are rising taxes for schools, water, and other essential services. Suburban sprawl, increased land costs, lengthened commuting time, inadequate transportation facilities, and massive traffic jams, have escalated to nettlesome problems. Recognizing the unsatisfactory trend of uncontrolled growth, public-minded individuals in and out of government have designed new patterns to redirect the expansion of suburbia, as well as the course of renewal in urban areas.

Regional planning considers the total environment of a large area and offers a blend of industrial, commercial, and residential facilities within the region. It is the first radical venture to avoid the hodge-podge development that characterized city growth in the past. Such uncontrolled expansion and incompatible land uses as the indiscriminate mixing of commercial, residential, and industrial properties are the main causes of deterioration associated with urban life. Urban deterioration is almost invariably followed by depreciating property values.

Although cities generally offer a greater variety of economic, social, and educational opportunities, they are plagued by congestion, monotony of continuous building bulk, noise, air pollution, and inadequate open areas for recreation. These conditions stem from failure to envision the impact of the total environment on the general welfare of inhabitants.

Advantages of suburban areas are more pleasant physical surroundings, more open space free of noxious air, less noise, and more privacy. The lesser variety of educational and cultural facilities in some suburban communities is offset by their accessibility to urban areas. Suburban spread, however, results in lengthening travel time and increased commutation costs.

HIGH RISK AREAS

Certain sections of the country are subject to periodic high tides, floods, and mudslides. Since properties exposed to these disasters are usually listed as uninsurable risks, the owners are compelled to sustain all losses. These areas should be avoided unless pressing reasons require you to live in any of them.

The canyon districts of southern California, for example, are highly susceptible to mudslides. Among the causes of these mudslides are severe brush fires that destroy vegetation and roots which clutch the soil and help resist the rapid runoff during torrential rains. Geological peculiarities in the Los Angeles basin have been further disturbed by construction of thousands of homes built on slopes ranging up to 45 degrees. In January 1969, houses priced from $35,000 to $50,000 were buried under massive layers of mud.

These grim tragedies are repeated because warnings of geological experts are unheeded. Dr. Donald Belcher, director of Cornell University's Center for Aerial Photographic Studies, has observed:

"Mudslides that have been occurring in California are perfectly natural appearances that are certain to occur, and which spread out over predictable areas."

Flood disasters are risks in regions where rivers become swollen by melting snows. The upper Midwest becomes inundated when mammoth Canadian snow packs melt under the spring sun. Time and again rampaging rivers have taken a high toll in property damage, injury, and death. Some towns, learning from past experience, have built dikes that have proved effective. But the lasting solution is to construct reservoirs and dams to hold back and control the unbridled rivers.

Before buying a home in an unfamiliar section, consult one or more insurance firms doing business in that state, since they compile careful records of all hazardous areas. Local newspaper files are also a reliable source of information. Casual inquiries among neighboring residents will often elicit useful knowledge.

THE COMMUNITY

Communities were traditional commercial centers that served people living in wide areas around them. All roads radiated from these business hubs. Streets in these growing urban centers developed in the gridiron pattern (Fig. 2.1)—avenues crossed by streets, all as straight as possible—to expedite movement of people and supplies to and from the commercial and industrial centers. Each block became a square island surrounded by four traffic arteries, with people exposed to baneful fumes, noise, and accidents.

The concept of cluster zoning (Fig. 2.2) is an attempt to solve some of these troublesome problems. Houses are grouped around expansive, commonly-owned space (Fig. 2.3). Winding roads and dead-end streets within the development allow children to walk to schools and playgrounds without crossing a main road. High schools and athletic fields are located away from any major through street, an arrangement affording safety without disrupting community traffic patterns.

Educational, cultural, and recreational centers are placed within the open space. A combined shopping and business center is clustered separately with convenient access for all residents. Cluster zoning saves on lot development costs because streets and sewer and utility

Fig. 2.1   Conventional Street Grid

Source—PUD, City Planning Commission, N.Y.

Fig. 2.2   Cluster Development

Source—PUD, City Planning Commission, N.Y.

lines are shorter. Grouped houses mean less bulldozing, leveling of land, and landscaping.

The "new town" is a form of total planning for a self-sustaining community. It incorporates every function essential to the daily lives of its inhabitants. Dwellings vary to suit multiple needs, and include

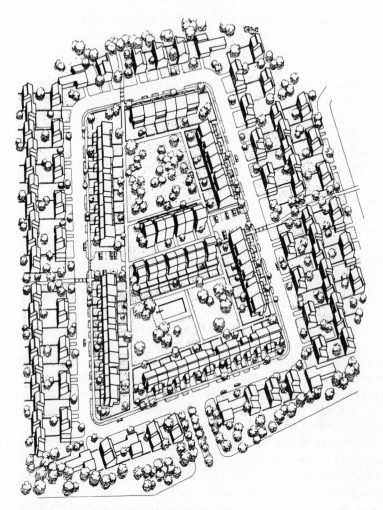

Fig. 2.3   Section of Cluster Development

Source—PUD, City Planning Commission, N.Y.

one-family units, semi-attached homes, row houses, and limited apartment buildings. Industrial and commercial enterprises are integral to a new town.

Since housing is designed for various income levels, a complete manpower pool is available. Irrespective of the town's size, people can live, work, and spend much of their leisure within its border. These "new towns," encircled by their own green belts or open spaces, have proved successful in England, Scandinavia, and West Germany.

Planned residential communities, often utilizing the cluster zoning principle, are more typical of housing developments in America. Homes in these communities are usually characterized by similarity in design and price, and almost invariably attract people of the same income level.

The ideal community offers its inhabitants maximum municipal services, such as schools, libraries, sanitation services, police, and fire protection, at minimal tax cost to the individual. Such economic stability is based on business and light industry paying taxes in excess of services required. These commercial enterprises add substantially to the community's economic soundness by drawing related secondary activities, manpower, and miscellaneous service establishments.

In residential communities that are part of towns, rising costs of local government are borne heavily by home owners.

To offset this burden, many communities created industrial councils to attract business and industry to their areas. As a result industrial "parks," aesthetically pleasing as well as economically productive, developed. Today most states and many municipal governments have departments of industrial or economic development. This pressure for strong economic bases will ultimately result in more self-sufficient communities in suburbia.

At present, homes in older communities are individually designed, compared to the sameness of dwellings in new developments. Lack of municipal and educational facilities are not so acute in established suburbs as in new sections. Unavailable vacant land in older areas helps restrain a large population increase. Improvements or additions to existing community facilities, even construction of new buildings, are less of a tax burden than in new communities where schools, sanitation services, and police and fire protection must be provided within a short period. These municipal expenses are reflected in the tax rate.

Inflationary costs in new communities also include higher assessed valuations, the basis on which real estate taxes are imposed. Older communities are similarly affected by high prices because their taxes are also raised. But homes in these areas started with a lower tax base or assessed valuation. Many older communities also have active civic and taxpayer groups to protect their interests, a weighty factor in community stability. Lacking such concern, communities may drift and eventually deteriorate.

Schools

Not surprisingly, a high proportion of home buyers select a community for the quality of its school system. School construction since World War II has scarcely kept up with the needs of new families. Some farsighted tract developers donate part of their land for school construction, occasionally including the building itself. Educational facilities reflect much of a community's character and often serve as centers for civic and recreational activities.

Questions and doubts about a school are usually resolved by consulting the local educators. They should be able to tell you how the achievement scores of their school compare with the national average. Standard achievement test scores indicate the efficacy of elementary school programs, just as scores on college entrance examinations reflect the quality of education in high schools.

Factors that contribute to a meaningful school system embody an individualized program with leeway for varying abilities of pupils; small class size; some allowance in budget for experimentation and innovation in teaching methods; an adequate school library; current expenditures per pupil (excluding cost of transportation or funds for new schools and equipment), which should not be below the national average; and a low rate of teacher turnover. A high percentage of teacher turnover is an indication that either salaries are too low or working conditions are unsatisfactory, or both.

Police and Fire Protection

An efficient police force is not necessarily a large police force. Although crime is steadily on the rise in suburban and rural areas (with burglaries in the lead), many communities are adequately protected by a small number of policemen, often serving only during part of the day or at night. Emergency assistance is usually given by state police. Although the latter are primarily concerned with highway traffic, crime, and accidents, they cooperate closely with local officers.

Residents who identify with their communities generate an awareness of incipient disruptive pressures and a pervasive mood that tends to restrain local potential lawbreakers. Active civic groups pinpoint likely trouble spots so that preventive action can be taken. Residents in such communities value their property rights and those of their neighbors. Privacy is respected, but there is an awareness of any unusual activity or strangers in the neighborhood. The degree of police protection required by any one neighborhood in a community depends not only on its residents, but also on the adjacent areas.

Many suburbs have introduced the "rescue squad" or ambulance corps manned by volunteers who augment the services of their police and fire departments. Schooled in first aid and rescue methods, these squads purchase, equip, and operate ambulances to provide round-the-clock ambulance service, without charge, to all area inhabitants. Many urban neighborhoods impressed by the success of these volunteer squads now offer similar services.

Communities not protected by professional fire departments rely on volunteers trained in fire-fighting skills who operate apparatus provided by the municipal government. Fire volunteers in many communities are granted special real estate tax exemptions. Fire insurance rates are an accurate index of protection in an area—higher safeguards lower the basic rate for home owners.

Sanitation Services

Refuse collection and disposal are indispensable to a community's health. Newly built and expanding communities usually impose a special charge for this service, or require home owners to hire private carters. Snow clearance in northern regions is provided either by a municipal department or by private firms hired by contract for this service. Street-cleaning services in suburban residential areas are generally minimal.

Municipal sewage facilities in both urban and suburban areas often are inadequate to cope with the needs of the expanding population. Many areas without municipal sewage disposal facilities must rely on private disposal systems such as cesspools and septic tanks (see p. 104–6). Indeed, there are districts in large metropolitan areas, such as New York City, which still lack municipal sewers.

Sewer lines, sewage treatment plants, and related facilities are expensive, and their costs are usually imposed directly on the property owners who derive their benefits. Where assessments for sanitation services are imposed on a community-wide basis, the cost is spread. Increased tax rates will reflect the cost of these improvements.

Because of the high cost of sewage disposal facilities, many home owners have resisted and frequently opposed their installation. But pollution of water supplies makes sewers and sewage treatment plants mandatory. To curb water pollution, some states have taken legislative action to force installation of these facilities.

State and federal grants that are available for these essential services must usually be matched by municipal funds, which some communities have difficulty providing. Because water pollution is a regional rather than a local problem, quasi-public sewerage authorities have been established in some areas. Funded by federal and state government loans, the authority assumes responsibility for providing and servicing main sewer trunklines and sewage treatment plants. Communities utilizing the disposal facilities pay a sewerage use fee which is passed on to the individual user. The authority uses the funds derived from these fees to repay the loans. Thus costs are spread over a long period of time and distributed over a wide regional area.

In some realty subdivisions, the developer installs a private disposal system serving all the houses on the tract. This facilitates the eventual construction of a public sewer system but, in the meantime, relieves the individual home owner of unnecessary expenditures for private facilities. Some communities require a private disposal system of this type before plans are approved for the subdivision.

A rapid realty growth in certain areas has produced serious health hazards. New Jersey, in a recent case, forced suspension of construction on several hundred new houses to forestall a health menace caused by inadequate sewage disposal. Many families were denied possession of new houses because of lack of sanitation facilities.

Water and Power Supplies

Water is still one of the cheapest commodities supplied by many municipalities, but acute shortages will adversely affect the economy of any area. In some arid western regions water is piped long distances and is expensive for the user.

Rainfall and snow run-off absorbed in the ground are prime sources of potable water. Water shortage studies focus attention on the "underground water table," the quantity of water stored in the ground and how far below the surface the supply is located. Underground water tables have fallen considerably in nearly all parts of America.

Open space and plant life are vital factors for adequate water supply. Rapid expansion in cities and towns demands more water, but facilities lag behind need. Wells are the water source in rural and suburban areas where municipal water is not available.

Mounting electrical needs often strain the capacities of public utilities, but no danger of serious shortages exists. These plants invariably manage to catch up with expanding demands. Private companies are the main source of electric power, but their rates are regulated by law. In sections using electricity supplied by governmental agencies, rates are generally lower and vary according to the proximity of power sources.

Transportation

Surge of growth is closely associated with availability of mass transportation and inter-connecting highways. Commuting time and fares are important considerations, as is parking space at bus and rail terminals. If you will drive to work, check traffic conditions at the hours you expect to be on the road. Availability of local public transportation will determine whether or not a second car should be included in your budget.

Recreational and Cultural Facilities

Former Secretary of the Interior Stewart L. Udall has indicated that, "No matter how urbanized we may become, we recognize the need for a contact with nature as the touchstone that gives meaning to our lives and purpose to our enterprises."

Parks, playgrounds, baseball fields, swimming pools, and other open recreational areas are important to the well-being of every community, whether it is a crowded city or a quiet suburb. In urban areas, parks and cemeteries are often the only green spaces in vast expanses of concrete and asphalt. Too frequently, lack of open areas, and the resultant adverse effect on the environment, is recognized only after all available land has been crowded with buildings. Municipal or other government agencies must then take expensive remedial action. This lack of foresight has also appeared in mushrooming suburbia.

A good portion (often as much as 50 percent) of the open space available in many cities and suburbs has been the result of private land philanthrophy. New York City, trying to make its environment more amenable, offers bonuses (usually permitting higher towers or making concessions on other regulations) to encourage builders to leave open sections, such as arcades and plazas, around their buildings. The value of open space should not be underestimated.

In a persuasive appeal for open space, the Open Space Action Institute in its report *Stewardship* has indicated that "Open space gives us a place to recreate—both in the active sense of sports and games as well as the passive pursuits such as hiking, observing nature, or just finding a quiet place. Open space provides the basic environment necessary for the proper development of children. It helps instill in them a responsiveness and respect for nature that comes only through an intimate contact with it. Open space gives, free of charge, a place for water to purify and to be stored for our use. It provides, in the form of forests and marshes, swamps and other wet places, a method of flood control more efficient and less expensive than any yet devised by man. Open space, whether a park, a nature sanctuary, a scout reservation or a buffer strip, adds to the value of private properties that touch its perimeters and increases the net value of an entire community as well.

"Thus we can defend the preservation of open space as a physical resource . . . not only for aesthetic and ethical reasons but also for hard-headed economic and social reasons."

Nearly all cultural and social facilities—museums, theaters, libraries, zoos, clubs, churches and synagogues—and other complexes to meet the needs of people can be found in urban areas. Many suburban and rural districts focus interest on one of these activities, such as music festivals, to draw people to their communities. Libraries, or library services, are found everywhere. Not all cultural and recreational activities are available in every community, but automobiles make these facilities readily accessible. Your special interests should be a factor in selecting a community for your home.

Medical Facilities

Medical centers are generally associated with universities in urban areas. In suburbia, voluntary hospitals frequently are the only facilities available for a large region. Doctors, dentists, and other medical people tend to congregate in urban areas. Some communities have tried equipping a building to serve as a medical center to attract professionals. In other areas, group practice has received wide support. Thoughtful consideration should be given to the availability of medical assistance.

Judging the Community

Professional developers have learned to evaluate a community by the attitude of its residents during conversational interviews. A community's stability or ebb depends largely upon the concern, disposition, and actions of its inhabitants. Pride in a community and its goals is reflected in civic participation. Use the gauge of professional developers: converse leisurely with people in the community where you plan to live.

THE NEIGHBORHOOD

Neighborhoods are as diverse as the people who live in them. Their confines may consist of one block, a sizable subdivision or, in the suburbs, an area encompassing several square miles. A neighborhood is characterized by such commonly shared features as streets lined with identical houses, an historic vicinity, or perhaps deteriorating buildings, or an area subject to a set of covenants that "run with the land," which are binding on each successive owner of the property.

The Home Buyer's Checklist, Appendix I, will help you evaluate the desirability of a neighborhood.

THE LOT

Lot size is usually a matter of personal preference—subject, of course, to zoning regulations. Those who have a "green thumb" may want a larger parcel of land, since they enjoy caring for a lawn and garden themselves. Others may have the financial means to hire a professional gardener for landscape maintenance during the spring and summer.

Few homes present a more inviting appearance than those ensconced in a fully landscaped lot with tall graceful trees, decorative shrubbery, and a thick carpet of green grass. Older trees protect the dwelling from the wind and shade it from the hot sun. In addition to beautifying the property, landscaping adds substantially to its value.

Besides its eye-pleasing effect, a larger front lawn affords more privacy from the street. Wide lawns and deep rear gardens provide privacy from neighbors. Many building codes specify the proportion of land that a dwelling may occupy. Any future plan to build an extension to the house may be contingent on the amount of land you have.

Many buyers prefer a corner house since it offers the advantages of more light, air, and space on wider, quiet streets. However, builders usually charge more for a corner house because it is on a larger plot. The former chore of shoveling snow from two sidewalks, considered a disadvantage of corner lots in northern areas, is now obviated by gas-powered snow blowers. Corner houses have two front lawns, but maintenance is generally minimal.

Drainage and erosion are important considerations in choosing a lot. A steeply sloped lot has little utilitarian value; it is also difficult to maintain. If possible, select gently sloped land which not only provides good drainage but can also be used for outdoor living. A lot at the bottom of a hill should be carefully inspected; it might lose its topsoil from descending cascades of water during heavy rainfall. If adequate drainage and storm sewer facilities are absent, seek your house elsewhere.

HOUSE ORIENTATION

Most communities restrict the size of a house and its placement, or orientation, on the lot. Even when an option is given, your plot should be large enough to allow for the most favorable position in relation to view, sun, climate, and prevailing winds. House orientation, particularly in northern areas, can provide more sunlight and warmth in winter, less condensation on windows, and lower fuel bills. In the summertime the house will be several degrees cooler.

Plans for house placement depend on the sun's shifting angle of elevation between summer and winter. When the sun descends from its high summer path to the low winter sky, it rises in the southeast and sets in the southwest (see Fig. 2.4). Only walls and windows facing this southerly direction will receive warming rays. Rooms where the family spends most of its time—the living, dining, and recreation areas—are best arranged for this exposure.

The kitchen in a rectangular house should be located for the same southern exposure. Since this is not always possible, alternative exposures are east or northeast. Desirable as sunshine is in the kitchen during winter, it can be unbearable later on when the hot summer sun is added to cooking heat. Morning summer sun in the east is usually beyond the kitchen's exposure by noon.

Many people prefer a bedroom that does not face the bright morning sunlight because it disturbs their sleep. Placing the room in the direction of the setting sun will obviate this annoyance. Early risers usually welcome the morning sun. Parts of the house facing west sometimes develop an oven-like temperature. But a garage at this end of the house will block much of the sun's heat.

Wide eaves or overhangs give good shade against the torrid midday sun, but are not effective against its low angle rays in the morning or afternoon. Eaves also allow windows to remain open during heavy summer rains. Tall, broad-leafed or deciduous trees

POSITION OF SUN AT NOON FOR LATITUDE 40° NORTH

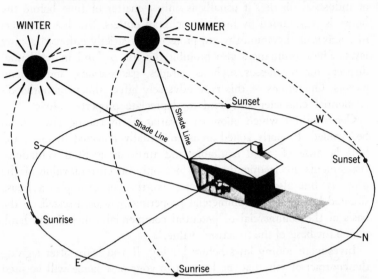

Fig. 2.4 Solar Orientation

on the east, west, and south sides make excellent summer shade. Their leaves drop off in fall, allowing the winter sun to shine through the bare branches. Spruce trees or evergreens on the north side will help shield your house against harsh winter winds.

Houses usually have at least two entrances. If feasible, neither one should face prevailing winter winds that often sweep into the house when the door is opened. Information on the direction of prevailing winds can be obtained from the local weather bureau. Essential considerations for orientation are lessened in insulated houses with full or partial air conditioning and double pane windows.

ZONING

Zoning ordinances were originally enacted to prevent crowded city areas from becoming more congested. These local laws also banned commercial or industrial operations that might cause fires or explosions. Such activities were permitted only in outlying areas, safely away from the populated center.

Almost every city, town, or village has zoning laws intended to protect the property owner. If a dwelling borders a commercial or industrial district, it usually is only a matter of time before the house is surrounded by factories or retail outlets. But home owners in a substantial community are protected by strictly enforced zoning laws. These ordinances also prohibit the use of land in residential districts for businesses such as garages, gas stations, and funeral parlors. Operations of this type adversely affect the neighborhood's residential character and tend to depreciate property values.

Communities which allow easy variances in zoning laws are to be avoided. Properly zoned areas are usually reflected in lower tax bills because of more equitable and uniform assessed valuations. Assessments are frequently based not only on current value of the property but also on the projected worth. For example, a house situated between two commercial properties may be assessed on the basis of the commercial or potential commercial value of the land, not on the basis of the structure's value.

Investigate zoning laws before buying. If you learn after signing the contract of sale that the lot next to your new home will be used for a bowling alley or gas station, as permitted by the zoning law, it will be too late to do anything about it. Every person who buys real estate is presumed to have examined the local laws concerning his property. These public records may be examined free. A copy of the zoning maps (Fig. 2.5) can be obtained from the county or town clerk for a nominal sum.

A mortgage loan is never granted unless the lender is satisfied that the property is not in conflict with zoning ordinances. Because a zoning violation may result in a lawsuit, the lender will avoid any involvement that might endanger his security—the house—for the mortgage loan. Your own attorney should advise you what restrictions are imposed on the use of the land.

Zoning laws may further dictate the community's residential character by prohibiting one-family homes from being converted to two-family dwellings, or by preventing the owner from using part of his house for business activities, such as a custom-tailor shop, that might affect the neighborhood's character.

A community may be zoned to require a minimum lot of two acres for each one-family dwelling. An outsider who buys a one-acre lot would be denied a building permit. Restrictions of this kind

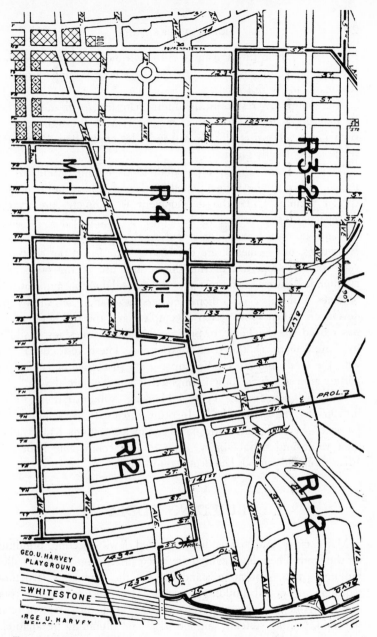

Fig. 2.5   Zoning Map

Key: R = Residence Districts   C = Commercial Districts   M = Manufacturing Districts

23

have been upheld by the courts. Although model zoning laws have been proposed in past years, present statutes still range from the reasonable to the ridiculous.

If a zoning law results in an undue hardship to the new owner, he may apply for a variance or modification of the ordinance. In such a case, a board of officials will study his application. Reasonable requests are usually granted.

New town and cluster type subdivisions require municipal approval, either in the form of modification of zoning ordinances or special permits. Once the development is complete, preservation of the open space is assured either by the municipal government or land use deed restrictions, enforceable in civil courts. Deed restrictions, or easements, are the best way to assure the continued value of the properties in the cluster and use of the open areas as intended. Every property owner in the subdivision automatically becomes a member of a home owners association set up by the developer. When construction is complete and the last home owner has moved in, the home owners association assumes responsibility for enforcement of the deed restrictions. These restrictions "run with the land" and are binding upon each successive owner in perpetuity unless a time limit is imposed when they are drawn.

A study made for the Federal Housing Administration (FHA) in 1965 by the Urban Land Institute disclosed that communities protected by such automatic membership associations had retained their value and marketability, even though comparable houses in adjacent neighborhoods had declined in value.

BUILDING CODES

Many cities and towns have enacted laws affecting buildings on the land. These laws, which are listed in separate volumes called building codes, determine standards for the numerous structural requirements of all buildings proposed for erection in the community. Among these requirements are kinds of fireproof construction, heating systems, and electrical and plumbing installations.

Because building codes are so complicated, no new construction should be undertaken unless the plan has been prepared or examined by an architect who is familiar with the local regulations. Codes are growing so complex that in many areas they are now divided into a building code, a plumbing code, and an electrical code.

Older homes are termed "non-complying" if they were built before the codes were enacted. This means that any major alteration of an older dwelling, especially the installation of electrical and plumbing equipment, will generally be required to comply with the current laws. Inspectors, local officials authorized to enforce the zoning laws and building codes, examine the construction or alterations during various stages of progress after the building permits have been granted.

When violations are discovered by the inspector, the owner is notified and given time to correct them. If these remain uncorrected, the owner faces penalties enforceable by the local authorities. Since a time interval usually exists between notice of violation and legal action by the local governing body, a prospective buyer should unfailingly have the municipal records searched to learn whether violations of record exist before the title is closed.

In the event of one or more violations, the buyer should notify and request the seller to correct any non-compliance at the seller's expense before accepting title. Some violations, such as defective electrical wiring, or a hazardous heating system, are expensive to correct. Here again, a lawyer's guidance is vital, since he will insert a protective provision in the contract requiring the seller to make these repairs at the seller's expense.

Chapter 3

Used and New Houses

Choosing a used house or new one is a puzzling alternative to many buyers at the outset, but an estimated 70 percent finally decide on an older home. Fewer than 30 percent buy new dwellings. Between 1 and 2 percent select custom-built houses designed by architects, or hire contractors to construct them.

ADVANTAGES AND DISADVANTAGES OF A USED HOUSE

Although older houses are generally less expensive than new ones, they are also likely to require more repairs. Many older dwellings, however, have been diligently maintained and offer more space, especially in the moderate price range. A large family in need of four or five bedrooms will select an older structure as a matter of necessity. A new house with this number of bedrooms is usually beyond the average family's purse.

Because the older house will be found in an established neighborhood, you can assess the value of nearby homes and the probable rise or decline in property values. Taxes are always less in an older neighborhood and seldom rise at the rate of real estate in newly developed areas. Exceptions are new homes constructed on occasional vacant lots in an established community Their base assessments for tax rates are higher.

Well cared for older homes are pleasantly landscaped—an important consideration, for new houses require topsoil, plants, shrubs, and trees. Viewing the surrounding neighborhood from the house gives you an opportunity to consider its attributes, including the architectural style and apparent condition of nearby dwellings. You can easily observe the condition of sidewalks, streets, and the amount of traffic. Explore the community to determine whether it has essential services—schools, playgrounds, libraries, sewers, good water supply, sanitation, and police and fire protection.

When you finally narrow your selection to the home that best meets your needs and price, remember that a used house is sold "as is," without any guarantees as to its physical condition. If you are doubtful about your expertise in house construction (see Chapter 6) and appraisal, professional help is available at reasonable fees. An appraiser, who has spent years acquiring his knowledge of property values in the area, will rate the dwelling on its location, its exterior and interior design, and its construction features.

Furthermore, the appraiser will carefully estimate the cost of replacement, then subtract an allowance for all physical wear and tear. Beginning with the neighborhood, he will examine schools, transportation, shopping, and related facilities. By weighing these factors against selling prices of similar homes in the immediate neighborhood, he will arrive at a fairly accurate estimate of the house's current market value.

Size and space do not always mean the same when applied to an older structure. Many of these homes were designed in a rambling fashion, resulting in considerable wasted space. Houses that are fifty years old or more reflect notions which are quaint by modern standards. Nooks and crannies added by romantically inclined architects are so much waste space today. Many of these houses were heavily ornamented with gingerbread exterior trim. But this type of house is often avidly sought by persons who have nostalgic sentiments. These houses often have spacious interiors. Exterior ornamentation is not a serious disadvantage. Stripped of its gingerbread, many a house will present clean, modern lines—but modernization costs are generally high.

Do not buy an older house solely because of its appearance. Although colonial houses had small, wavy window panes, they were not intended as a picturesque attraction; glassmakers simply were unable to make larger and smoother ones. Architectural fashion of past generations left much to be copied and adapted to modern design. But a contemporary and efficient domicile demands space flexibility and interior arrangements unknown to the hardy colonials.

Even houses of more recent vintage lack the compact arrangements of newer homes. High construction costs today compel builders to convert every square foot to practical use. When looking at a home, note its usable space in relation to your needs.

When inspecting an older house, bear in mind that some improvements are comparatively inexpensive, such as storm windows, painting, or enclosing an open porch. But installing a new boiler or adding a bathroom is costly. The local utility company will inform you, without charge, about the electrical system and how much work is required to update it to meet modern needs. Expenses for these and other repairs should be added to the purchase price of the house to determine its actual cost.

The cause of defects in one house is not always applicable to others. Repairing structural faults may be high-priced in one but comparatively inexpensive in another. Some defects are visible, others are not. One dwelling may be old, faded, and shabby in appearance but structurally as strong as the day it was built. Others may be new in years but severely defective structurally.

ADVANTAGES AND DISADVANTAGES OF A NEW HOUSE

New homes are usually multiple-built units on a tract of land acquired by a builder. With some exceptions there is little difference in price among the units; the range is narrow, resulting in communal parity. This is an important consideration in tracts of traditional gridiron patterns. Cluster zoning and new town developments preclude total economic homogeneity.

Previous arrangements by the tract developer with the Federal Housing Administration and banks simplify mortgage applications and approvals. But real estate taxes can be only estimated, not fixed, until all homes are built and general needs known. In most cases taxes are markedly higher than estimated by the builder. As new services are needed, taxes will continue to rise.

Exercise caution when buying a tract house. Your decision will be based on a display model, invitingly decorated and advantageously placed. Builders routinely set their show house amid spacious, expensive landscaping, but this feature is not necessarily included in the price, nor is the elaborately embellished interior designed by a professional decorator. Dazzling fixtures and other appurtenances are extra. These may add several thousand dollars more to the price of the home. Do not accept verbal promises. Unless you have the builder's assurance in writing, listing all items that go with the house, you have no legal claim against him even if he reneges on every detail.

New homes usually carry a year's guarantee against defects, during which time the builder will make any necessary adjustments and repairs. Damage caused by careless use is not included.

Prices for new houses are usually firm. Little, if any, latitude exists for the bargaining that is common when buying an older home. Dickering is possible only when the builder is unable to sell at his initial price and is pressed for money.

THE CUSTOM-BUILT HOUSE

No existing house, new or old, can meet a family's needs more perfectly than a custom-built home. But it will be some time before you and your family agree on all details and can convey your thought to the architect who will prepare a preliminary plan. After more thought, discussion, criticism, and perhaps argument, the final blueprint will be ready. This improved plan will include the architect's suggestions and recommendations. He is a specialist at contriving the utmost space for every dollar spent.

Despite this optimal arrangement, custom-built houses represent only a small percentage of all one-family construction in the United States. Cost is the main obstacle. Architects' fees range from 6 to 15 percent of the total price, depending on the project's size and complexity. A home designed in this manner must be sufficiently expensive to have an architect accept your project. Even a 15 percent fee on a $30,000 dwelling is scarcely enough to pay for his time and office expenses.

Whatever money the architect may save you through dealing with the builder and expert choice of materials, his fee must be added to the ultimate cost of the house. Before an architect agrees to design and oversee the erection of a custom-built home, he will compute the amount of his fee.

The title "architect" denotes that the individual has proved his professional competence by official examination, and is licensed by the state to practice his profession. An architect performs the following services: He will consider your family's needs in relation to your budget for the house. If you have no site in mind, the architect will advise you on selecting one in the best possible location. A preliminary sketch, or general plan, is drawn and includes tentative cost estimates. Then a complete plan will be submitted depicting the entire house, floor plans, structural details, exteriors and mechanical installations—all drawn to scale. Builders and contractors will be selected on the basis of bids and reliability. At this point, the architect can be given full supervision of the project, or you can deal directly with the contractor.

If the architect is retained to see the job through, he will have all work done to comply with the plans and specifications. He will review proposals by the contractor for substitution of materials, or changes, then advise you in writing. Unless the contractor receives his "change orders" in writing, he cannot depart from the agreement. A thorough inspection of the work done is made by the architect before making final payment for the finished house.

Before employing an architect, be sure his concept of house design agrees with yours. In your preliminary discussions, ask him to let you examine photos and drawings of houses he has designed. Visit them to examine their appearances and structural quality. A candid discussion with the owners will be helpful to you in reaching a decision.

If no architect has an office in your area, you will have to pay more to one who has to travel back and forth. Your bank is often a good source to consult about an architect. The Federal Housing Administration allows lending agencies to include an architect's fees when granting a loan.

A custom-built house will provide you with extras that a tract builder cannot furnish. Your architect will recommend specifications with an eye to the future, such as water pipes of larger diameter than standard size, and more amperage including heavier electric wiring than currently required. Costs of these materials will be slightly higher at the outset, but such changes in later years would cost much more to make.

When planning with your architect, consider a turn-around space for the driveway. In northern areas an electric heating system under the driveway saves snow shoveling chores. Merely flicking a switch will melt the heaviest accumulation of snow. Other specialized features are radio-controlled garage doors and storage space in the garage for garden and sports equipment.

STOCK HOUSE PLANS

Stock plans are mass printed, inexpensive house blueprints sold by magazines published for homeowners, mail-order firms, construction material dealers, and an occasional department store. These architect-designed plans seldom cost more than forty dollars, usually less. They must be bought in several sets for contractors who are asked to submit bids. Plans include a list of materials and specifications for their use.

Unless you can read blueprints, understand specifications and the quality of different materials, and can differentiate a well-planned design from a mediocre one, you may incur a very costly risk in using stock plans. To rely on recommendations of the contractor or lumber dealer, who are not architects, is at best shaky assurance. Every change made will add to the expense. Neither publisher nor distributor will give cost estimates, which can be obtained only by securing bids from several contractors. Construction prices for the same stock plans will vary in different sectors, depending on cost of materials and labor. Mortgage loans are not readily given for this type of project.

FHA MINIMUM PROPERTY STANDARDS

Among the advantages of a Federal Housing Administration insured mortgage is that the approved structure must meet the agency's "minimum property standards." FHA approval before construction of a new house protects the buyer against major defects for up to four years. Under this guarantee, you are entitled to seek redress. Congress enacted this law in 1963, following widespread abuses by dishonest builders.

Applied to an older house, the FHA's minimum standards reduce, but do not prevent, the likelihood of buying a defective structure. Although hundreds of items are included in the FHA checklist, not all are of the best quality. Many of these are required to meet only *minimum* standards. In examining a used house, the FHA inspector considers only its age and cost. He will not evaluate the house above FHA's basic standards. The responsibility to know the house's architectural, structural, and utilitarian qualities devolves upon you.

Chapter 4

Types of Houses

ONE OR MORE LEVELS

The architectural styles of modern dwellings are borrowed from various sources. Within the many variations are four basic types: the Cape Cod or cottage; the bi-level or two-story; the split-level or one-and-one-half, or two-stories at slightly different levels; and the ranch style or one-level.

The Cape Cod

Shortly after World War I, the Cape Cod (Fig. 4.1) became one of the most popular styles in America. Named after the wind-swept peninsula at southeastern Massachusetts where it was first built in the late seventeenth century, the Cape Cod is specifically designed to withstand the bone-chilling, north Atlantic winter and is constructed around a large central chimney. Unlike homes with exterior chimneys, the warmth emanating from the flue made the Cape Cod easy to heat. In an area where wood is not plentiful, this was an important concern.

Built close to the ground along simple lines, the Cape Cod has neither a full second story nor a roof overhang. The roof pitch was designed to prevent a pile-up of snow, and the high ridge

Fig. 4.1 Cape Cod *Source—Johns-Manville*

Fig. 4.2 Cape Cod with Dormers   *Source—Master Plan Service, Inc.*

adds only a half-story to the structure. The Cape Cod can, however, lend itself to various extensions and alterations, while still retaining its distinctive style. It can be built at comparatively low cost and maintained at less expense than most other frame dwellings. The need for additional space produced dormers (Fig. 4.2) that were placed in the roof to provide extra room and light. Many a Cape Cod roof is literally raised to accommodate growing families.

The Bi-Level

The bi-level is a two-story structure designed to provide an equal amount of living space on each floor. Bedrooms on the upper floor afford much more privacy, since visiting and other household activities are customarily confined to the lower level. This type of dwelling costs less per square foot to construct than a sprawling ranch house. It requires less land and less roof area, which results in other savings.

The colonial two-story (Fig. 4.3) derives its name from the style of house which appeared along the eastern seaboard of the United States in the eighteenth century. Georgian style homes were more elaborate and built for the wealthier colonists, who were impressed with the red brick, white-trimmed mansions developed in the reigns of England's four Georges. Dutch colonial style is characterized by the gambrel roof (Fig. 4.4), allowing full conversion of the attic to another livable floor.

Extensive ornamentation in bi-level houses, generally called Victorian architecture, was introduced in post-Civil War years. The Victorian structures were decorated with cupolas, balconies, porches, and stained glass windows. The high narrow tapered gables and turrets in round, square, and octagonal shapes gave this style the appellation of gingerbread. The exterior trim was in scrolls and fretwork to an extent limited only by the designer's imagination. No interior was complete without embellished ceilings, carved moldings, and heavy wooden posts. The extravagances of this architectural style were possible because highly skilled artisans often worked for a pittance.

English Tudor-style houses became popular during the late 1920s and are found in many northern suburban areas. These sturdily built

Fig. 4.3   Colonial Two-Story   Source—Master Plan Service, Inc.

Fig. 4.4 Dutch Colonial—Gambrel Roof *Source—Johns-Manville*

dwellings are typified by half-timbers set in stucco and brick. High construction costs and scarcity of masons skilled in stucco work now restrict this style to the custom-built market.

Location of the stairway in a bi-level seems unimportant to some builders. But a center hall and stairway, common in colonial design, is preferable to a side hall entrance. Living and dining areas are separated by a center hall, and the kitchen conveniently leads directly to the dining area. With a side hall entrance, it becomes necessary to walk across the living room to reach the stairs. Wall areas in the living room are then broken up with numerous doors and windows which present problems in interior decoration. Although the bi-level offers more living space on smaller lots, climbing stairs can be onerous for the elderly and infirm.

The Split-Level

Although it was originally designed for a hillside, the split-level (Fig. 4.5) can be built in such variations as the front-rear split and the side-to-side split. This type of structure is ideally suited for uneven terrain. In a front-rear split (Fig. 4.6), the front of the house is on one level and the rear on another level; a side-to-side split (Fig. 4.7) has one side of the dwelling on a different level from the other side. The split-level has become so popular that bulldozers often are used to build an artificial hill on which this style house can be erected. In recent years a modification of the split-level has been built on level land, and today the term is also applied to houses with short flights of stairs leading to different interior levels.

Treading up and down the different short flights of stairs to reach various rooms can be wearisome. Furthermore, heating the split-level house can be difficult and costly. Large open stairways at different levels allow heat from one room to disperse into an upper one. Only zone heating (p. 114), where each level is zoned to pipe heat as needed into its area, will adequately warm such a house.

Fig. 4.5   Split-Level House   *Source—House & Home*

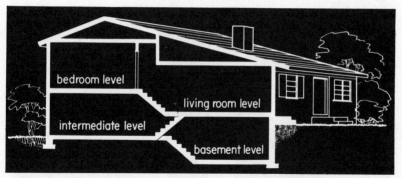

Fig. 4.6 Front-Rear Split-Level *Source—Master Plan Service, Inc.*

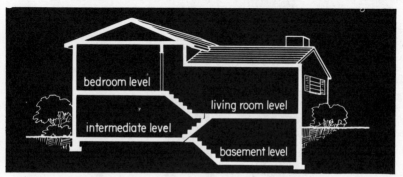

Fig. 4.7 Side-to-Side Split-Level *Source—Master Plan Service, Inc.*

The Ranch House

The ranch house (Fig. 4.8) is becoming a national style. It is an ideal domicile for those who shun stairs, because all rooms are on one level. Before World War II, about two-thirds of new one-family homes had one level. By the middle 1950s, seven-eighths of new buildings were the one-level ranch style. Today this is the type of dwelling most people prefer.

A ranch house requires more land and costs more per square foot than other kinds of one-family structures. This is due to larger roof area, longer foundation walls, and the addition of ells. The true ranch house has no basement. Utility or laundry rooms are on the same level as the living quarters.

To serve its true purpose, a ranch house must be spacious enough

Fig. 4.8 Ranch House *Source—House & Home*

to allow movement and privacy on the same level. Many ranch homes are too compact to afford these facilities. They are, in effect, small private apartments that become increasingly abrasive as expanding families encounter less privacy. Because of lot size limitations in some suburban areas, expanding a ranch house can prove to be an expensive proposition unless some foresight is exercised at the time of construction.

Numerous ranch houses built today have basements. Some builders also include an expansion attic that may be finished into one or more bedrooms. Reverting to three levels, this "ranch" has a basement, main floor, and an expansion attic.

As land has become more expensive, some builders have produced what they call a "hi-rise" ranch house. This type of home has a basement at grade (street) level which includes a garage, utility room, and frequently a recreation or family room and a powder room or bathroom. Although labeled a "ranch" because all main living areas, living room, dining room and bedrooms are on one floor, it is actually a bi-level structure. Because no excavation is made for the basement, the hi-rise ranch does not present the low lines considered characteristic of ranch houses. Placed next to a conventional bi-level house, its height becomes visually incongruous. Within a development of identical houses the design is more acceptable. Although none of these variations is a true ranch house, builders have learned that the term has good sales value.

THE PREFABRICATED HOUSE

A prefabricated dwelling, or prefab, is manufactured in components that are partially preassembled in the plant and shipped to the site for erection. This package includes finished exterior walls with windows, roof and floor sections, interior partitions, and kitchen cabinets. How much more you will get, including appliances, depends on price. The trend seems to be toward more complete house units, embracing every part except concrete and labor used on the site. Since labor represents the largest cost in house construction, prefabs can be built more economically at the factory, where volume buying and improved production methods are computed with considerable accuracy.

Prefab manufacturers offer a variety of styles designed by their own architects and including contemporary, bi-level in colonial and Dutch colonial styles, ranch, and Cape Cod. Variations within these basic designs are also available. Quality of materials has improved substantially in recent years. Construction schedules are faster than those for conventionally built homes. After the foundation is placed, this type of house can be erected within several weeks. Some prefab manufacturers include heating, plumbing, and electrical systems. Most, however, prefer to have these installed on the site to conform to local building codes.

About 30 percent of all one-family houses built are prefabs. The Home Manufacturers Association, consisting of prefab makers, predicts at least 50 percent of all one-family homes erected by 1975 will be "factory built."

Prefabs range in price from about $8,500 to more than $200,000, but most are sold for less than $15,000. Because the prefab itself represents only a small part of the total cost to the homebuyer, you should determine in advance what is included in the price. Additional costs are price of the site, the excavation, the foundation, then erecting and finishing the structure (which includes wiring, heating, plumbing, and landscaping).

Mortgages on prefabs are treated routinely by lending institutions. FHA or Veterans Administration (VA) loans apply as they do for other dwellings. Both agencies are familiar with the structural qualities of prefabs. A number of manufacturers maintain departments that arrange for FHA, VA, and conventional mortgages. Lending institutions generally make no distinction between prefabs and standard dwellings.

Prefab manufacturers readily admit that their homes cease to be competitive when they must be shipped beyond 500 miles, because shipping costs wipe out the cost difference. Some contend prefabs can be shipped economically up to twice this distance. These claims can be easily checked against prices of comparable housing units.

The Home Manufacturers Association, Room 1117, Barr Building, Washington, D.C., will provide prospective buyers with *A Fact Book on Home Manufacturing* plus a list of manufacturers and their areas of distribution.

SHELL HOUSES

Unlike a prefabricated house, the "shell" house shipment arrives as precut but unassembled lumber and is not ready to live in when erected. It is an unfinished house shell, consisting of little more than exterior walls, roofing, rough flooring, windows, and doors.

This type of semi-finished construction appeals to those prospective home owners more or less skilled in carpentry, who can save considerable money by performing most of the labor themselves. Since the houses are without plumbing, wiring, or heating, the buyer will have to install these himself or employ a contractor. Before buying a shell house, you should check the zoning laws and building codes to ascertain whether this type of structure is permitted.

Shell houses are sold on the assumption that the buyer owns the lot on which he plans to build. Prices are generally so low that no down payment is required. But mortgage financing for such projects is difficult and expensive. Furthermore, much depends on the buyer's carpentry skill, and for those who lack such skills and money, finishing a shell house may be an impossible ambition. Thus only short term loans from five to seven years are given, at exorbitant rates, because the house may never be completed. Interest rates discounted in advance may amount to 15 percent or more.

Only a few shell houses conform to FHA minimum standards. Most shell houses are intended for rural sections without protective building codes.

ATTACHED AND SEMI-ATTACHED HOUSES

In districts near urban centers, where land is expensive, semi-attached and attached or "row" houses are popular. In this type of construction common side walls need no exterior finish, windows, doors, or insulation. These houses, which range from 16 to 20 feet wide, are often lacking in spaciousness but the heating and cooling costs are low. The major economy is savings in land cost. Lot-to-lot houses require no side yards, less area for sidewalks and streets, and less expense for power lines.

Suburban developers have learned that row houses sell faster if they are called "town houses" or "patio houses." Where zoning laws permit, builders erect two-family row houses which are bought by people with limited budgets. The two-family arrangement enables many owners to defray the mortgage and other costs by rental of the second apartment.

With only pocket-size front yards and no side yards (but some space in the rear), occupants have limited outdoor living space. Lack of garage space is another disadvantage. A garage in this narrow building can usually accommodate only one car. Row house developments in tracts farther from the city usually have more common open space because land is less expensive.

Semi-attached one-and two-family houses share a common wall, and each has a small side as well as a rear yard. Ownership of a semi-attached house can be a nuisance if one owner's color scheme for his portion of the house clashes too violently with his neighbor's. It is not easy to sell this type of home if one-half is kept in good condition and the other is badly neglected.

Chapter 5

Interior Plans

FLOOR PLANNING AND
FAMILY TRAFFIC PATTERNS

In the early 1950s the concept of "togetherness" was populaıized in countless newspaper and magazine articles. Inevitably, builders applied this term to interior layout, eliminating some walls or building them only four feet high. Aside from making small rooms appear larger and saving construction costs, this type of planning made it imperative for families to see more and more of each other. Togetherness afforded the privacy of a dormitory.

Lack of adequate partitions aggravated the problem of noise. For some time, home improvement contractors thrived by installing walls that should have been erected with the house. Still mesmerized by this economical method of construction, some builders issued "surveys" purportedly to prove a majority of buyers preferred "open interior space." But unsold houses slowly persuaded builders that no further profit could be extracted from togetherness.

Humans are indeed social animals, but they are distinguished from other species by a need for privacy at times, even from their families. Good traffic planning ensures privacy by devising floor plans to permit different kinds of activities without interfering with non-participants. Rooms for family or group activities include the dining and recreation areas. Work areas are the kitchen, laundry and sewing room, and the shop for carpentry and related maintenance tasks. Allowances should be made for areas for private activities, such as studying, dressing, sleeping, or for just being alone.

Access to bathrooms or other zones of activity should not require passage through any private area. Living rooms are not intended for through traffic, and poor planning that converts them into a family passageway should be avoided. Common sense planning controls family traffic to the kitchen from the front and rear entrances, dining room, bathroom, and laundry; from living room to dining room, and from living room to bedrooms and bathrooms. Builders of new tract houses will often revise existing plans to meet your particular needs at little or no extra charge, provided no structural changes are necessary. A non-load bearing partition, one that does not brace any part of the structure above it, can be rearranged with no difficulty. But if the partition supports an upper floor, an alteration is expensive.

If floor plans of your prospective house are unavailable, you can make your own with tape measure, pencil, and graph paper lined with squares. Available in various rulings, a convenient graph sheet has four squares to an inch. By allowing each one-quarter inch square to equal one foot, an accurate small scale plan can be drawn, including location of windows, doors, and closets. If you make such a plan for every home under serious consideration, you can study and compare them more critically.

Family needs vary with size. An eight-member family obviously requires more space than a family with only two children. Less room for private activities is required in homes where all children are of the same sex or very close in age. Casual and unconstrained families will easily dispense with a formal dining room, using it rather as a combined recreational-eating area.

Stairs are most conveniently located in the center of a house so that no one must pass through another room to reach them. Short flights of steps between rooms interfere with smooth traffic flow and are a cause of home accidents. Steep and narrow stairways, particularly circular ones, are the poorest design, and, besides being tiring, they are hazardous to both young and old.

Low headroom over stairways is another casualty source, frequently causing bumped heads. Headroom should be at least $6\frac{1}{2}$ feet. Good

planning includes correctly proportioned steps so they are not uncomfortably steep or dangerous. Stair treads should be at least 10
inches wide, and the risers not less than 7½ inches high nor more
than 8 inches. And no stairway is actually safe without handrails.

In a properly proportioned room, the length should not exceed
twice the width. When possible the relation of length to width
should be less. Many architects have been critical of square rooms,
but sometimes a nearly square room affords a more interesting interior
arrangement. L-shaped rooms for living and dining, or sleeping and
dressing, have provided new conveniences.

ROOM FEATURES

In choosing your house, pay attention to the little things that can
make such a difference to your comfort. Actual room size can be
irrelevant if wall space is broken by too many windows and entrances. Space under low windows is virtually unusable. Furnishing
the room which has much broken wall space is a difficult task, even
for a professional decorator. Abutments or obstructions, such as
protruding radiators, further complicate the decorating problem. Un-
broken and sufficiently large wall areas should be available to accommodate the large pieces of furniture required for that particular
room and provide more flexibility for furniture arrangement.

Properly located light switches should not be concealed behind
open doors. Nor should electric outlets be centered on walls where
they will be blocked by large pieces of furniture. When looking at
a home, notice the location of overhead and wall lights, switches,
and the number of outlets in each room.

Open areas that lack doors are merely passageways, space stripped
of privacy. As you open doors, note whether they strike other open
doors. Check door widths to see if all your larger items can be
carried through. If a room can be entered only through a narrow
hall, you will be severely limited in your choice of furnishings.

A thoughtfully designed dining unit permits the table to be set
without disturbing other contiguous areas. There should be ample
room to carry in and remove dishes and food.

Bedrooms, too, should have enough space to accommodate beds

conveniently and to allow easy and efficient movement. Sometimes rooms are so poorly planned or so undersized that space for movement is confined to a single footpath.

THE KITCHEN

Outdated kitchens are common in older homes that have not been modernized. Simply looking at the refrigerator, stove, and counter and storage areas will reveal whether they are adequate to serve your family's needs or whether they must be replaced. Modernizing these units is relatively expensive.

Home economists agree that there are four possible kitchen plans,

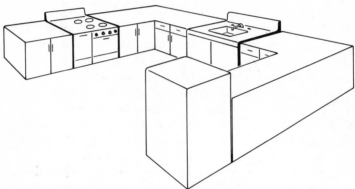

Fig. 5.1   U-Shape Kitchen

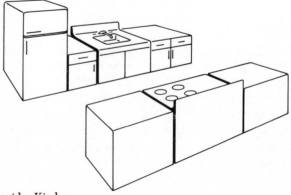

Fig. 5.2   Corridor Kitchen

depending on the room's shape and size, and placement of doors and windows.

The U-shaped kitchen (Fig. 5.1) has work centers on three walls: the sink at the center, preferably under a window, the range and oven on one side wall, the refrigerator on the other.

The two-wall or corridor type kitchen (Fig. 5.2) is an arrangement with appliances along parallel walls: the range and oven on one side, and the refrigerator and sink on the other.

The L-shaped layout (Fig. 5.3) has all appliances and cabinets along two adjoining walls: the range and refrigerator are on either side of the sink.

In kitchens with only one usable wall, all appliances are in a row with the sink in the center (Fig. 5.4).

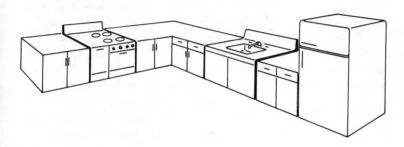

Fig. 5.3   L-Shape Kitchen

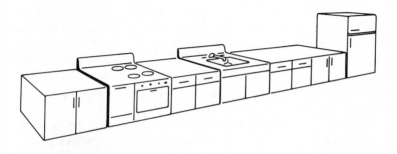

Fig. 5.4   Single-Wall Kitchen

Whichever arrangement exists, good lighting is essential. A poorly located kitchen light, blocked by someone standing at the sink, casts a shadow on the work area.

Work surfaces on both sides of the sink, range, and refrigerator facilitate efficient preparation of meals. Counter tops should be covered with material that resists heat, stains, and mildew. Among the most commonly used products, linoleum is low in price but is damaged by some alkalis and shows scorch marks and heat rings. Vinyl is a thermoplastic with greater resilience and resistance to most food stains, but it dents easily and costs more than linoleum. Ceramic tile is expensive, cracks under impact, and is not worth the higher cost.

Laminated plastics cost more but are tough and durable. These resin-impregnated sheets are sold under such trade names as Formica and Micarta. Laminates are also used for cabinet and wall panels. Although they are almost impervious to acids, alkalis, and alcohol, they can be discolored by intense heat. Laminates are available in a wide variety of colors and patterns. A backsplash of laminate along all work areas, including the stove, will protect the wall from grease and stains, and is easily kept clean.

Without ample storage cabinets, no kitchen can be efficient. Cabinets are available in a large variety of metal, wood, hardwood, and plastic laminates, and their finish usually influences the kitchen's color scheme. Despite many complaints about lack of cabinets, surveys usually indicate the contrary. Food packages, bags, and jars randomly placed on shelves result in wasted space. Thus upper shelves often remain unused because they are hard to reach. A combination step stool on casters will make this storage space easily available.

A built-in ventilating fan will quickly exhaust cooking odors, heat, grease, smoke, and water vapor. The fan should be near as possible to the range. A metal hood over the range will direct fumes to the exhaust duct. During cold weather an average kitchen produces up to twelve pounds of moisture daily. In houses without vapor barriers (p. 109), condensation will permeate exterior walls, causing paint and wallpaper to peel away, and eventually rot the wood.

Filter hoods without exhaust fans are available but are not adequate substitutes. Odors are absorbed by charcoal traps which must often be cleaned of grease and dirt. Exhaust fans and ducts, too, must be cleaned, but they are much more effective air fresheners. Fans are sold in eight and ten-inch sizes. Even if your kitchen is small, select a ten-inch fan with two speeds. It moves more cubic feet of air at minimal difference in power cost.

A kitchen should have two entrances, one near the driveway or garage for convenient access when bringing in groceries, and another leading to the dining room. The main floor washroom, or half-bath, is best located in the entrance hall leading to the kitchen.

BATHROOMS

A well-planned interior includes a master bedroom with its own bathroom. Other bathrooms should be located where they can be reached from any area without passing through another room. Every floor should have a bathroom. A half-bath, which consists of a water closet and washbasin, is adequate on floors with no bedrooms, such as the main level and basement.

Bathrooms rank high as accident zones in the house. Many accidents can be prevented by installing hand bars on bathtub and shower stall walls. Vertical hand bars, from floor to ceiling, in front of a bathtub are essential for the aged and infirm. Non-slip materials placed on the bottom of the tub will increase the safety factor.

Hot and cold water outlets should be controlled by thermostatic mixing valves to prevent scalding. Devised to provide an even flow of water at any desired temperature, the valve can be operated safely even by a child. Steam or hot water radiators should be covered to protect against accidental burns. Faucet handles and towel bars should be of stainless metal. Glass and porcelain have a tendency to break in jagged pieces and may make deep, lacerated wounds.

The light switch is best located on the latch side of the door where it cannot be reached by anyone standing in the tub or shower. Many persons, particularly children, have been badly shocked or electrocuted in this manner.

Bathrooms are easier to maintain when the walls are tiled to at least 54 inches above the floor. Ceramic tile is traditional for this purpose, but plastic tile is a good substitute at less cost.

Inspect the tub, sink, and toilet bowl for proper installation; joints should be smoothly cemented without evidence of leakage. Be sure the fixtures are not chipped. Another desirable fixture in a bathroom is a combination light, infrared heater, and ventilation fan, enclosed in one unit that can be operated separately or jointly.

THE BASEMENT

A waterproof basement with adequate headroom is an asset. Houses with livable basements always command a higher price. A finished basement is an excellent family recreation room. A basement can be subdivided to include a laundry, a workshop, and hobby and storage areas.

Older homes had no basements but cellars, often with a dirt floor, where coal was stored along with other clutter. Those who occasionally looked to this level for extra living space were discouraged by coal dust. As oil replaced coal for heating, the basement assumed new meaning for growing families. Many basements, however, were not designed to provide livable space, and require expensive structural alterations if they are to be converted to such use.

Low ceiling height is a common drawback. A ceiling should be at least 7 feet high if the occupants are to be spared the feeling of being confined in a narrow, crowded space. In houses with basements lacking headroom, the floor must be lowered by excavation. Columns or posts that support the girder cannot be shifted or rearranged. Remodeling must be done around them. Sometimes the posts can be neatly concealed in a wall partition, or by having a bar or hutch designed around them. If a partition actually supports the upper floor, no change should be made until another support is constructed.

No attempt should be made to finish a wet or damp basement until it is waterproofed (p. 64). If the basement lacks windows, their installation is optional. New lighting design and air-conditioning may satisfy all requirements for a comfortable atmosphere in a windowless basement.

Manufacturers of prefabricated wood panels, drywalls, acoustical ceiling tiles, and lighting fixtures provide useful design and installation guidance to home handymen who plan to finish their basements. Alternatives to wall partitions are free-standing room dividers made of shelves and poles, translucent plastic panels, and similar decorative materials. Almost indestructible epoxy enamel in a variety of colors will give masonry floors and walls a very hard, durable finish. Indoor-outdoor carpeting squares can also be easily installed.

Surveys show that young families outgrow basementless houses much sooner than those who have this extra space. The overwhelming preference for a home with a basement is demonstrated by the willingness of buyers to pay more for a dwelling with this convenience. A basement with a separate entrance helps keep the upper floors clean; children can go directly to it without tracking mud through other parts of the house.

THE GARAGE

Where there is a choice, a garage is best located on the west side of a house to shield the home from the hot summer sun. The garage may be attached to the structure or connected by a covered pathway to allow convenient and protected passage to or from the car during inclement weather. The garage should also be close as possible to the kitchen to lessen the burden when toting groceries from the car.

Garage driveways that descend steeply from the street are not desirable. Water may run into the structure during drenching rains, and snow and ice accumulation can create winter hazards. The preferred driveway slopes gently away from the garage. A long driveway may mean more snow shoveling in the winter. If you have no alternative in this matter, a flame thrower can be used to melt snow and ice. These devices, which are available through large mail order firms, shoot a flame at 2,000 degrees, and, when used with *caution*, will quickly clear your driveway.

A driver-controlled electronic device to automatically open or close a garage door is a convenience, particularly in stormy weather. By pressing the button of a solid state transmitter in the car, a silent signal is relayed to a power unit in the garage which raises or lowers the door. The average transmitter operates within 75 feet of the garage. More powerful units are available for longer distances. Transmitters certified by the Federal Communications Commission are unaffected by other electronic devices or passing aircraft.

PATIOS, TERRACES, AND DECKS

American families have enthusiastically turned to the use of patios, terraces, and decks for outdoor living space. Originally the patio was a courtyard or inner area, exposed to the sky, a popular feature of Spanish and Spanish-American architecture. Patios may or may not be paved. Terraces are unroofed, paved areas immediately adjacent to the house, and overlooking a garden or lawn. The words "terrace" and "patio" are now used interchangeably.

Terraces and paved patios should be constructed along the same principle as the slab in a basementless house (p. 63) but no waterproof membrane is necessary. The most serviceable terrace is made of concrete laid on a bed of sand and small aggregate, reinforced with thick wire mesh. It may be surfaced with flagstone, bluestone, bricks or other types of masonry. Alternate freezing and thawing in northern sectors cause many poorly constructed terraces to heave and buckle every spring.

Patios and terraces are usually unroofed, but screens of wood slats, reed fencing, or canvas or plastic panels are frequently used to provide privacy and protection from sun and wind.

Decks are used to provide outdoor living space for rooms above the ground floor, or where construction of a patio or terrace is not feasible because sloping land would require extensive grading or an expensive retaining wall. Deck construction is of a simple type, similar to that used in boardwalks. Posts are set in footings and support beams covered with planks which form the deck. Decks can be built in multiple levels. The spacing between planks permits rainwater runoff. The most suitable woods for decks are redwood, cedar, or cypress; but any wood used close to the ground should be treated with a wood preservative. Unroofed decks have replaced the old-fashioned porch as an architectural feature.

If the house has a terrace or paved patio, observe its condition and pitch for rainwater runoff. Water should drain away from the house.

STORAGE SPACE

Select your house with an eye to storage facilities. The requirements for storage space will vary with family size, social activities, and climate. More space will be required in cold regions for winter clothing and sports equipment. Families who entertain frequently need extra closets for the convenience of guests. Those who travel, fish, or pursue hobbies must have more space for luggage and other paraphernalia.

FHA minimum storage standards are 75 cubic feet of closet space for each bedroom (3'½" x 3' x 7' is 73½ cubic feet). Two hundred cubic feet are required for the average house, exclusive of closet space. Homes without attics or basements promise little future storage space accommodation, unless a room or more is added.

The entrance closet should be large enough to hold outer clothing, umbrellas, rubbers, and other articles of outdoor wear. Some homes now include a "mud room" near a ground floor rear or side entrance, where wet and dirty garments may be shed before one goes to other parts of the house.

Twin closets in the master bedroom for individual use by husband and wife are especially desirable. Separate storage space should be available for the numerous toys and other items amassed by children.

A linen closet, located close to the bedrooms and bathrooms, should be large enough to provide storage for sheets, towels, blankets, and extra pillows, as well as such miscellaneous items as heating pads and boxes of tissues. Broom closets also require ample space to store cleaning aids such as floor waxers, mops, vacuum cleaners, carpet sweepers, and brooms. If the dwelling has a family or recreation room, it should have enough storage space for all articles and equipment used in this area.

Garments, leather luggage, and similar articles should not be stored where contact with heated surfaces, such as radiators and chimneys, is possible, because under this condition these materials will deteriorate rapidly. Ventilated storage areas prevent odors and mildew, particularly in damp climates. In extreme cases, a dehumidifying heater will be effective.

Light fixtures installed in closets and storage spaces will prevent groping and accidents. The National Electric Code (p. 88) requires light fixtures to be installed only on the ceiling in a closet. Wall lights become a fire hazard when clothes remain in contact with them.

SPACE FLEXIBILITY

When looking at a house bear in mind that only a custom-built home will completely satisfy your immediate and future requirements. Seek the home that will meet most of your needs, but which has space flexibility to accommodate your family's changing requirements. Space flexibility simply means that rooms or other areas can be adapted easily for multiple use or readily changed to meet new requirements.

If the dwelling has a basement and attic, you will not encounter critical future storage problems. Extra storage space can also be found in part of the garage, even dead space within partitions, for shelves and cabinets.

Chapter 6

House Construction

Used or resale homes are sold on an "as is" basis, meaning that whatever defects occur or are discovered after the transfer of the property are solely the responsibility of the new owner.

In new homes the builder usually gives a year's guarantee against defects in materials and workmanship. Many new homes, however, may develop serious defects after the guarantee expires. An eager builder, anxious to sell his houses, is a decidedly obliging fellow. But after the contract is signed, the ardent salesman becomes a very reluctant dragon. Other builders set up corporations which somehow disappear or go into bankruptcy after the last house in the development is sold.

Except for homes in the upper price range, the majority of new houses are built on a production line basis. Most building is in suburban areas, where a developer acquires large tracts of undeveloped land. About six to ten standard plans are used in this type of construction. By varying the designs slightly, the builder erects what appear to be twenty-five or more kinds of dwellings.

After foundations are mass poured, other work crews lay the flooring, erect the frame, etc. When the first few houses are completed at least one is furnished as a model house, at which time they are advertised. Examining the models permits the prospective buyer to determine the overall construction and finish.

Many builders save a great deal of money by constructing smaller rooms, which are then furnished by interior decorators skilled in the art of optical illusion. Mirrors are used generously to convey a sense of spaciousness. Smaller-sized furniture especially designed for limited space or children increases the deception. Many families move into new homes only to discover unhappily that their furniture does not fit. Carry a retractable steel tape when inspecting model homes. You may be amazed to learn that an apparently 12' x 16' master bedroom is actually several feet smaller.

Not many prospective buyers are sufficiently familiar with basic construction to discover all the needed repairs. Carry a copy of the Home Buyer's Checklist (p. 225) as a general guide for detecting major defects and to record your observations. If the house still impresses you as worth purchasing, you may decide to have it examined by a professional house inspector who will provide a written report for a fee ranging from forty dollars to sixty dollars for most houses.

Private home developments have one or more model homes to attract buyers. Contracts for such dwellings contain the tricky clause "similar to," which legally allows the builder enough leeway to defraud the trustful buyer. A knowledge of basic house construction (Fig. 6.1) will enable you to specify better materials before signing the contract.

Sometimes attention to small items can mean large savings. Wood shingle siding fastened with iron nails, for example, becomes rust-streaked after a few years. If you insist upon aluminum nails before signing the contract, the builder will agree. Rustpoof nails will save hundreds of dollars in painting costs. At a moderate additional cost you can substitute durable aluminum or vinyl gutters and leaders for short-lived galvanized steel, and heavier roofing shingles that will outlast, by several times, those included in the builder's standard materials.

You'll want to be familiar with these

BUILDING TERMS

1. Gutter and downspouts
2. Louver for ventilation
3. Horizontal (lap) siding
4. Insulating sheathing
5. Brick veneer
6. Grade line
7. Header
8. Corner post of three 2x4s
9. Waterproofing
10. Drain tile
11. Foundation footing
12. Foundation wall
13. Sill plate
14. Sole plate
15. Joists
16. Rough diagonal flooring
17. Finish flooring
18. Insulation
19. Collar beam rafter support
20. Ridge
21. Chimney flashing
22. Clay tile flue lining
23. Asphalt felt layers
24. Top plate
25. Studding
26. Asphalt paper
27. Structural beam
28. Bridging
29. Lally column
30. Wood roof boards
31. Asphalt shingles

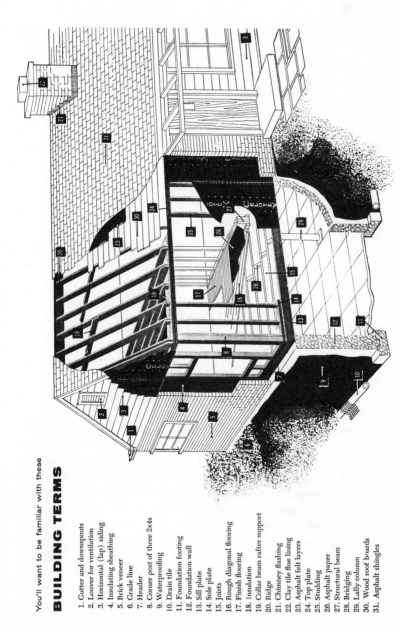

Fig. 6.1   Basic House Construction   *Source—The Celotex Corporation*

61

THE FOUNDATION

Footing

A house may have no basement but it is never without a footing
(Fig. 6.2), the concrete base on which the foundation rests. Footing
size should comply with local codes. A dependable method is to
make the depth of the footing equal to the thickness of the foundation wall, and its width should extend one-half the wall's thickness
on either side. Thus a 1 foot foundation wall for a one-level house
could safely rest on a footing 18″ wide and 12″ thick. For a two-
story dwelling, a footing 24″ wide and 12″ thick provides a good
margin of safety.

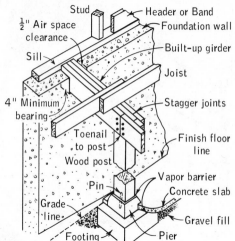

Fig. 6.2
Lower Structural
Members

Footing depth depends on the latitude where the frost line varies
with climate. The frost line is the limit below which the soil does
not freeze, ranging from a depth of about 6 feet along the northern
border of America to zero or ground level in the sub-tropical southern
regions of Florida, Texas, and California. A footing not below the
frost line will heave and buckle under the earth's pressure as the
ground freezes and thaws seasonally. This is a major cause of
cracked foundations and walls, and badly slanted floors.

Specifications for depth and dimensions of a footing are explicitly
defined in local building codes, but the negligence of an inspector
may wipe out the homeowner's investment. New York City's Build-

ings Department provides a calamitous example. In 1959 about twelve low-income families, who had saved for years to escape from their decrepit tenements, moved into a row of attached brick houses. About six months later, the three-story dwellings began to sag in the swamp on which they were built. Cracks, wide enough to admit daylight, appeared in the walls, and the floors tilted dangerously. Within several years the buildings were ruled unsafe and ordered demolished. A board of inquiry learned that the piles on which the footings rested had not been driven to sufficient depth. With only a fragmentary knowledge of construction methods, the Buildings Department inspector had been unaware of this blunder.

A court judgment against the builder was worthless because, following the guideline of all dishonest builders facing a judgment, the company was dissolved in bankruptcy. Suits against New York City, charging negligence by its Buildings Department, were dismissed by the court. The dozen families have irretrievably lost all they invested in the defective structures.

Besides underscoring the need for a firm footing, loosely filled ground should be compacted; all tree stumps and other pieces of lumber should be removed; and marshy soil should have deep-driven piles to prevent eventual structural collapse. A house on firm footing shows no perceptible settlement. The application of a waterproof membrane of asphalt-saturated felt over the soil will assure a dry basement floor.

Types of Foundation

Poured concrete makes the strongest foundation wall. Concrete blocks reinforced with vertical and horizontal iron rods require more work but are satisfactory. A new type of concrete block molded around a steel core made from discarded auto bodies reportedly withstands pressure greater than that of poured concrete. Cinder blocks are not acceptable in good construction. Besides lacking strength, their porosity allows excessive water seepage. Block foundations should be waterproofed.

A properly poured concrete slab base in a basementless dwelling is at least four inches thick, reinforced with heavy wire mesh or iron rods, and rests on four or more inches of gravel and sand. This aggregate provides excellent drainage. Water does not cling to sand as it does to soil. In freezing weather water-laden soil solidifies and expands, exerting much pressure against concrete. But sand acts as a cushion against this pressure.

In some houses foundation cracks, often near the base of a chimney, may result from unequal settling. In this case, the walls and ceilings on the upper floors will show similar cracks fanning out from the chimney's corners. Fine hairline cracks are no cause for concern, but wide ones indicate considerable uneven settlement. While searching for loose plaster near the chimney, tap the walls as you walk around each room. If large pieces of plaster are loosened from the lath, the entire wall may need replastering. (This defect can also result from other conditions not connected with a settling chimney.)

Crawl Space

The space in a basementless house from 18 to 36 inches high between ground and understructure, in which one can enter to make repairs, is defined as a crawl space. In damp areas where wood is subject to rot, ventilation is essential in a crawl space and also a ground moisture barrier of asphalt-saturated felt or a similar waterproofing membrane. A closed, heated crawl space in winter will prevent wood decay. In this case, the inner side of the foundation should be insulated.

Basement

If your house has a basement, inspection of this area can be most revealing. The concrete floor should have a sound surface and a gentle slope toward the drain. It is very important that a basement be free of water penetration through walls and floor. Rainwater should be drained by proper outside grading. Sometimes defective gutters and leaders allow the run-off water to dribble down the house walls.

Telltale signs of a wet basement are characteristic stains on the floor and walls, including cement flakes. Inspect the sills, joists, and girder for evidence of rot by jabbing an awl in these members. Wood must be wet often and for long periods before the softness of decay sets in. Prior to this stage the wood becomes discolored, moldy, and has stains caused by the fungi which flourish in moist wood.

Damp areas on the floor or walls do not always indicate leakage. In humid locations, particularly during damp summer days, condensation forms when inside temperatures are lower than those outside. A glass of ice water "sweating" on the outside is an excellent example. Ventilating the basement or briefly heating it will eliminate such dampness.

Some wet basements are caused by poor drainage around the house due to constant soil saturation. This condition is almost invariably indicated by a damp, musty odor and water marks along the lower part of walls. Improperly graded soil around the house can cause such seepage. The surrounding ground should slope away from the foundation.

A dwelling located in a picturesque dale will almost certainly be plagued by a wet, unusable basement. Rainwater from the surrounding higher land flows downward in underground streams, building up pressure against the foundation. It then passes through the porous masonry into the basement. If this condition remains uncorrected, the alternate freezing and thawing may crack the wall.

Installing a drainage system around the footing is effective. This is done by shoveling all the soil away from the foundation down to its base, and laying a drain tile along the footing. Damp-proofing the walls with either asphalt or pitch-base materials, before back-filling the soil, will add to the security of a dry basement. Houses on land that is higher than the surrounding terrain generally have no wet basement problems.

CONSTRUCTION LUMBER

Sold by grade and size, lumber is commercially divided into softwoods and hardwoods. Softwoods are evergreen trees whose needle-like leaves are retained in winter. Hardwoods are deciduous, broad-leafed trees that shed their leaves every autumn. Sometimes these terms are confusing; basswood and poplar are hardwoods, but their wood is much softer than that of Douglas fir or southern yellow pine, both softwoods.

Hardwoods are selected for appearance and suitability for furniture, paneling, and floors. Softwoods are largely used in construction where only strength is essential. A small volume of clear softwood, however, is used for trim and flooring. Grading is based on stress characteristics, such as density, stiffness, and defects. Softwood yard lumber is classified as Select or Common, each of which is further graded for knots, blemishes, and other defects.

Select lumber may be clear or slightly blemished. Common lumber has flaws in varying degrees that limit its use to construction and general utility.

The widespread practice of counterfeiting softwood lumber for building and remodeling was disclosed by the Federal Trade Commission (FTC) after a two-year investigation: "The masquerading of low grade lumber for high grade lumber has bilked consumers of millions of dollars and has lowered the margin of structural safety in innumerable dwellings; and, in the affected market areas, has impaired competitive mores among surviving wholesalers, retailers and contractors."

In its report to Congress, the FTC offered evidence that inferior lumber in houses lacked strength to support the stress placed upon it. Among cited examples were five developments in Long Island, New York, where in some 500 houses "at least 60 or even 70 percent of the lumber used . . . bore a fraudulent grademark stamp." Builders had to add double beams and joists to hold up sagging floors. The lumber used was utility grade but was stamped "Construction." The spurious grading is done anytime or anywhere after the lumber leaves the mill.

Because "low grade lumber is difficult to sell when marked, when falsified it commands a premium," the FTC added. Deceptive upgrading accounted for a "substantial share of lumber sales" in heavily populated areas such as California, New York, Texas, and Washington, D.C. Referring to the absence of any law against this larcenous practice, the FTC recommended: (1) The marking of softwood lumber should be made mandatory by trade regulation. (2) Laws should be enacted to ban the simulation and counterfeiting of grademarks, and make the knowing misrepresentation of species, size, grade or strength of lumber illegal. (3) The Federal government should inspect the grading and grademarking practices of softwood lumber distributors.

Home owners need not wait until laws are enacted. If you plan to buy a new house in a development, know and inspect the grades

TABLE 1

SOFTWOOD GRADE CHART

Select lumber is graded alphabetically. Common lumber has special grading names. (It was formerly graded numerically.)

SELECT LUMBER	GRADE	COMMON LUMBER	GRADE
Generally clean wood, used for flooring and trim.	A	Watertight lumber with limited blemishes or defects. Knots are tight. No waste.	CONSTRUC-TION
Few minor blemishes. Both A & B suitable for natural finishes with varnish, lacquer, or shellac	B	May have large, coarse defects. No waste.	STANDARD
Has surface imperfections that are easily covered by paint.	C	Large coarse knots, holes, and some decay. Used for concrete forms; sometimes sub-floors in low-priced homes.	UTILITY *
Has about five times more knots than Grade B. Used in low-priced houses for shelves and similar purposes.	D	Noticeable areas of decay; large knotholes. Much waste. Cleaner parts used for crates.	ECONOMY

* When utility grade common lumber is used for joists, it must be doubled to equal the strength of Standard or Construction grades. But good building practice precludes such use.

of lumber used (see Table 1). Even in a completed house, the beam, joists, and sometimes the studs, are usually exposed in the basement. Apply the same visual test to lumber in every remodeling or improvement job. Insist that the contract specify the grade of lumber to be used, and you will probably get the quality you expect.

BEAMS

A basement inspection properly includes an examination of the girder or beam, the main support of the structure, that extends the width of the dwelling along the basement's center. It may be of wood or steel. The latter is much stronger and can sustain a heavier load over a longer span. Steel girders are now commonly used in better-built houses. In structures without a basement the upper floor is supported by a load-bearing wall perpendicular to its joists.

Most older homes have a wooden girder as the principal support. A solid 6 x 8 or 8 x 10 inch timber is perfectly serviceable. In newer construction, this unit usually consists of three 2 x 6, 2 x 8, or 2 x 10 inch boards nailed together. Lacking the strength of a unified (or solid) beam, this type of built-up beam is satisfactory if the parts are arranged so the joints rest on the posts.

A wooden beam is always supported by either wooden posts or round metal Lally columns which resemble thick pipes. The Lally columns' hollow centers are usually filled with cement for added strength. Wooden posts are subject to rot or termite infestation. Probe the lower parts with a sharp icepick or awl. If the tool pierces the wood easily, the post should be replaced.

WALLS

Exterior Walls

The outer walls of a frame structure consist of sheathing or the first covering and the exterior finish or siding (Fig. 6.3). Besides forming a flat, rigid base for the siding, sheathing adds strength and insulation to the house. It is nailed directly to the studs, thereby bracing the frame as a unit. Many cheaply built homes in the South and West have no sheathing.

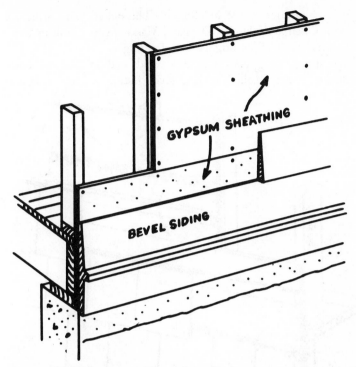

Fig. 6.3   Siding   *Source—The Celotex Corporation*

Typical sheathing materials are tongue and groove or square-edged boards, plywood, and combined sheathing-insulation panels. Diagonal sheathing is more expensive and if carefully done will enable the house to withstand fierce windstorms. This type of construction is extensively used in the Midwest and other tornado areas.

Lumber sheathing, which is never airtight, is covered with asphalt-saturated felt or a water-resistant building paper to protect the house against cold drafts and moisture. This is not necessary on sheathing-insulation panels that are encased in their own protective paper.

Finished outer walls are available in a variety of materials. Clapboard siding consists of boards, six to eight inches wide, tapered to a bevel or feather edge at the top. When clapboards are fitted snugly against each other, driving rains and wind cannot pass through. Normal maintenance and a coat of paint every few years enable this type of exterior to last indefinitely. The oldest frame structure in America, Fairbanks House, Dedham, Massachusetts, built in 1636, still retains much of its original wood siding.

Cedar shingle (Fig. 6.4) is another wood used on exteriors. Only the thicker variety, called shakes, gives lasting service. Asbestos-

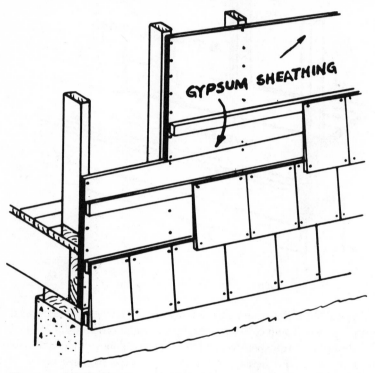

Fig. 6.4   Wood Shingles   *Source—The Celotex Corporation*

cement shingles, imitating wood grains, are fireproof but will fracture under impact. Newer siding materials are vinyl in solid colors, and white-enameled aluminum.

Careful nailing is essential if siding is to serve its purpose and not be ripped off in a windstorm. When inspecting exterior walls, note whether the joints, particularly at the corners, are tight and firm.

Masonry veneer walls (Fig. 6.5) are more expensive, but if properly constructed require less maintenance than other types. Solid brick or masonry walls are not built by tract developers. They are constructed only for the custom-built market. A veneer wall is the

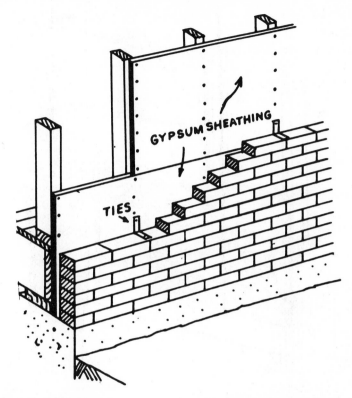

Fig. 6.5   Brick Veneer   *Source—The Celotex Corporation*

thickness of one brick; masonry is cut stone, called ashlar. Simulated stone is available at much less cost than ashlar masonry.

Bricks are rectangular clay blocks fired at cherry-red heat for several weeks. There are two types of building brick, common and face. The former includes all kinds of red brick without a finish. Every brick factory produces common brick from ordinary clay found in the vicinity. Its standard size is 8 inches long, 3¾ inches wide, and 2¼ inches thick.

Face brick—sometimes called tapestry brick—is molded from selected clays and heated longer for hardness and resistance to weather. Glazed brick has the added quality of being waterproof. Various blends and shades of red, blue, tan, and brown are found in face brick.

Crumbling mortar joints and cracks are the most common faults

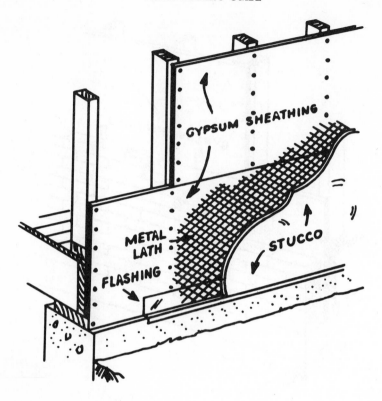

Fig. 6.6   Stucco   *Source—The Celotex Corporation*

in masonry veneer. Mortar that has fallen away can be replaced by pointing—that is, filling the joints. But cracks at different places or bulges indicate the wall is poorly secured to the sheathing. This can be corrected only by removing the wall and building a new one, using rust-resistant corrugated metal ties, one end nailed to the sheathing, the other laid between brick courses.

If a diagonally cracked brick wall rests on a fissured foundation, repairs will be very expensive. Defective brick walls on a sound foundation need not be replaced with new brick veneer. Any of the standard siding materials will give the house a new look at lower cost.

Stucco (Fig. 6.6) is a rigid curtain of cement held to the sheathing by galvanized lath. Any rough textured masonry surface, such as concrete block, can be used as a bonding base for stucco. Besides offering a high degree of fire protection, the insulating properties of stucco keep a house cooler in summer and warmer in winter. Stucco is a mixture of portland cement, sand, and water. Sometimes hydrated lime is added for greater ease in troweling.

Hairline cracks in portland cement stucco are common in cold climates, where heated interior walls expand. But these can be easily covered with special water-base thick stucco paints in matching colors. Large cracks can also be repaired if the metal lath is intact and firmly fastened to the wall.

At one time magnesite stucco was widely used. Magnesium compounds, mixed with sand and asbestos, in time corroded the metal lath, flaked, and crumbled. Even portland cement stucco applied over the defective surfaces is unsatisfactory. Portland stucco has a characteristically solid sound when tapped with a wooden object, but magnesite sounds hollow.

Very few stucco artisans work on frame houses today. Furthermore, it takes about six times longer to stucco a house than to attach standard siding. Most stucco work is limited to one- or two-story commercial and industrial buildings.

Interior Walls

The materials used to cover framed interior walls and ceilings are plaster and drywall, or gypsum wallboard. Plaster, a mixture of lime, sand, and water, must be applied wet in three separate coats on lath nailed to the studs. Lath formerly consisted of wooden slats nailed to the studs, but now metal is required by many local building codes because of its fireproof quality. A lath has many openings through which the first plaster coat is extruded, forming the base for the other two coats.

The first layer of plaster is called the scratch coat; after the plaster has set slightly, it is scratched so the second coat will bond securely. The second coat levels the work, and the third coat provides a smooth white finish. Gypsum board with ½ inch perforations is also used as a plaster base.

More expensive than drywall installation, plaster work is now largely confined to apartment and office buildings. In addition to high labor cost, plaster takes about a month or more to dry. During this time other workmen cannot proceed with their tasks. Builders of one-family homes routinely use gypsum wallboard, even in relatively expensive homes.

Plaster walls are preferable because they absorb sound more effectively and add rigidity to the structure. But use of insulating material with drywall helps to reduce noise. Drywall, also known as plasterboard, is made in 4 x 8 foot sheets with recessed edges. After being nailed to the studs or ceiling joists, their joints are filled with cement and covered with tape. The resulting smooth surface is then ready for paint or wallpaper. Wallboard in $\frac{1}{2}$ inch grade should be used for satisfactory installation. Thinner $\frac{3}{8}$ inch sheets are used by builders who practice corner cutting.

Severely cracked and broken plaster walls in older houses can be satisfactorily covered with wallboard to save the expense of new plaster construction. Applied directly over the defective wall, the sheets are secured to the studs by extra-long nails.

Another durable wall covering is handsome hardwood paneling in distinctive wood grain patterns. Protected by polyurethane and other synthetic resin finishes, these 4 x 8 foot panels are highly resistant to scratches. They can be installed directly over the studs, sound plaster, or wallboard, and are fastened by nails or cemented.

SOUNDPROOFING

Sound is more penetrating in homes built of lighter and unsubstantial materials. Bare walls and ceilings reflect and intensify noise, as do all hard surfaces. Rooms with large glass areas are particularly resonant. The clatter of today's heavy appliances intensifies noise in the home.

Soundproofing (acoustical) materials are soft, porous objects that have high sound-absorbent qualities. Among these are rugs, carpets, curtains, draperies, upholstered furniture, even people gathered in a room. Manufactured acoustical products consist of cellulose fibers, mineral or glass wool, cork granules, and similar substances which absorb and dissipate sound.

Acoustical tiles, available in attractive colors and patterns, can be stapled to furring strips, and nailed or cemented to the ceiling. They are very effective in recreation areas, kitchens, workshops, and other rooms with highly sound-reflective surfaces. Insulation between walls is also helpful in soundproofing a room.

THE ROOF

A well-designed roof will support heavy loads of snow and ice, and is sloped or pitched so that melted snow runs down quickly. The nearly flat roof is cheaper to build in a frame house, but is a weak load-bearer. Widely used in commercial buildings as well as homes, the flat roof is actually slightly pitched for proper water drainage. Unless strongly built, flat roofs are not desirable in northern areas where they may collapse under the weight of snow and ice. Making it strong enough to resist collapse under excessive weight would add considerably to the structure's cost.

Modern architectural style, however, often favors flat roofs, which are common in southern and southwestern states. They complement the simple lines that typify modern dwellings. But such roofs must rest on heavier joists to support their own weight.

Components for a pitched roof are less complex than those needed for other parts of the house, but more skill is necessary to assemble them; lumber must be cut precisely so that all angles and joints fit neatly into a unified framework.

Architectural styles of different periods are most readily identified by roof design. Colonial New England roofs were steeply pitched to shed snow. The gambrel roof, a variation of the gable, is Dutch colonial in design. The hip roof, of French provincial origin, is still popular but not the mansard, which also originated in France.

A roof line that sags lengthwise—along its ridge—deserves careful inspection. If the roof frame is partially collapsed, repairs will be extensive and expensive. Sometimes an owner of means, to gratify his whimsy, designs the roof with a low, curving sweep. Relatively few artisans today have the skill to do this type of work.

Drainage

Gutters and leaders (downspouts) should not be omitted when inspecting the roof. Their purpose is to protect the walls and to channel rainwater from the roof to a safe distance from the foundation; sometimes to a dry well in the ground or onto a concrete splash pan. To be effective, gutters must extend along all horizontal eaves. Repairing badly leaking gutters is a waste of money, since the condition indicates that other parts will soon corrode. Leaking gutters should be replaced.

Gutters and leaders are made of several materials. Copper, especially when coated with lead, is extremely durable but expensive. Aluminum and vinyl plastic are less costly and are very serviceable. Wood or galvanized gutters, which are found on many newer homes because the builder has cut corners to increase his profit, are the least satisfactory. Their troughs must be painted almost yearly to last beyond their normally short usefulness. In terms of long life, aluminum or plastic are less expensive.

Roof Coverings

Most roofs are covered with asphalt shingles. Manufactured in several types, shingle weight is based on the number that will cover 100 square feet of roof area. FHA minimum standard for this covering is the "235 pounds-per-square." But more lasting are the 250 to 300 pounds-per-square shingles.

Self-sealing asphalt shingles in the heavier weights provide added protection against strong winds and hurricanes. Dabs of black cement that bond under the sun's heat keep each shingle cemented down to the other and prevent them from breaking or tearing loose. Light color shingles have become increasingly popular—and for good reason, because they reflect the sun's torrid rays and help keep the house cooler.

Underwriter's Laboratories rate the best asphalt shingles Class "A," the hightest test rating awarded to roofing material (Fig. 6.7). These fire-safe and self-bonding shingles are guaranteed by their manufacturer for twenty-five years. Shingles last markedly longer in northern areas where their exposure to the hot summer sun is of shorter duration than in the South.

Slate shingles, available in thicknesses from $\frac{3}{16}$ to $\frac{3}{4}$ inch, have a weight of 700 to 2,500 pounds per 100 square feet. Because slate is heavy, sturdy roof construction is necessary. Although slate is more expensive than asphalt, it lasts indefinitely and maintenance is limited to occasional replacement of cracked slate.

Asbestos cement and clay tile give lasting service, but some types may soften and crumble after years of exposure. Red clay tile is

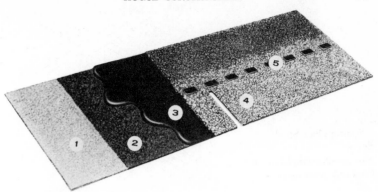

Fig. 6.7   Class A Shingle   *Source—Johns-Manville*
Legend:

1. Long-fibered felt base
2. Base felt saturated with asphalt to provide bond for coating asphalt.
3. Heavy coating of asphalt fortified with asbestos to provide secure base for granules and waterproof barrier.
4. Ceramic granules, embedded in the asphalt coating to provide shield against sun and resistance to fire, weather, and wear.
5. Self-sealing adhesive factory-applied to the face of each shingle. Sun's heat forms strong bond to make shingles storm-tight and wind resistant.

popular in warm countries and is easily replaced; however, its life is often limited in cold climates with much snow or ice.

Wood shingles were widely used at one time but are increasingly restricted because they are a fire hazard. In localities where this type of roof is not banned by the building code, fire insurance is usually unobtainable. But the code restriction does not apply to the use of wood shingles for exterior walls.

Copper is the oldest and most durable roofing material used. This expensive metal is most often seen on public buildings such as cathedrals. A well-laid copper roof will last at least a century. Some London buildings still have the copper roofs that were installed in the eighteenth century.

Flat roofs consist of alternate layers of roofing felt and asphalt or tar. The top layer is coated with small gravel or marble chips,

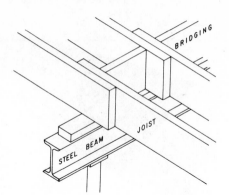

Fig. 6.8
Bridging Over Steel
Beam
*Source—National Forest
Products Association*

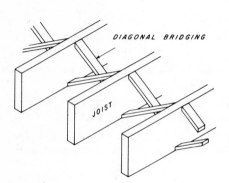

Fig. 6.9
Diagonal Bridging
*Source—National Forest
Products Association*

Fig. 6.10
Solid Bridging
*Source—National Forest
Products Association*

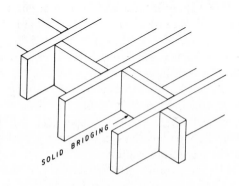

usually white, to reflect the sun's heat. A hot mopped roof is made by swabbing melted tar or asphalt over three or five layers of roll roofing.

FLOORS

Floors are supported by joists—horizontal framing planks, usually 2 x 8 or 2 x 10 inches in size. Placed edgewise on the sill in parallel series, joists are braced with bridging (Fig. 6.8)—short pieces of wood or metal nailed diagonally (Fig. 6.9) to them. Solid bridging (Fig. 6.10) consists of single blocks placed at right angles to the joists. Besides stiffening the joists, bridging holds them in permanent alignment and prevents warping.

In older structures the sill is a 4 x 6 inch wooden beam resting on top of the foundation walls, but in newer homes the sill is made of two 2 x 6 inch boards nailed together. The main supporting girder is level with the sill, and joists are laid across these major supports.

Wood flooring is manufactured in several types. The most widely used and least expensive is strip flooring. The better quality, tongue and grooved, resists buckling, a problem sometimes encountered with square edged strips. Flooring strips in shorter lengths are specially cut for high-priced installation in special designs such as herringbone.

Block or parquet flooring is made in two types—unit and laminated squares. The former consists of strips fastened together. The laminated block is formed by cross-grained layers. Like plywood, it is greatly resistant to moisture and there is less shrinkage or swelling. Blocks are cut in several sizes—$6\frac{3}{4}$ x $6\frac{3}{4}$ inches to about 12 x 12 inches. The size most widely used is 9 x 9 inches. The floor is usually laid in mastic.

Plank flooring is wider than strip flooring and is cut in random sizes. Better quality planks are cross laminated, a process similar to the fabrication of plywood, to resist warping. A popular method of installing this type of floor is to counterbore and fasten it with screws, which then are covered by wood plugs.

Most wood flooring can be obtained either prefinished or unfinished. Unfinished wood must be sanded, sealed, then finished with shellac or varnish, and polished. Surface appearance determines grade. Secondary grades have slight blemishes or defects.

About a dozen woods are used in flooring, half of which are hardwoods such as red and white oak, maple, birch, beech, and pecan. Softwoods used are southern pine, Douglas fir, western hemlock, western larch, and redwood. Only southern pine and Douglas fir are hard enough to give satisfactory service. Redwood's decay resistance allows it to be used for porch, deck, and other exposed floors. Hardwoods have greater resistance to wear and are generally more distinctive in graining.

When examining a house, walk over the floor slowly to determine whether it yields or squeaks excessively. Stand in the center of the room, rise high on your toes, and drop hard on your heels. A solid thud indicates that the floor has been securely laid over a subfloor and adequate-sized joists. If the floor vibrates excessively, you may be certain that the builder skimped on materials.

Floor Coverings

Kitchen, bathroom, and playroom floors may be covered with linoleum, or with asphalt or vinyl tile, the last being the most durable. Tiles should be checked to determine whether the joints fit snugly and are smooth and whether they fit properly around fixtures and in corners. Chipped and cracked pieces will permit water to seep under the base and loosen the tile from the floor.

Non-wood floor coverings are available in various materials. Asphalt tile contains less asphalt than resinous binders, plasticizers, asbestos, and color pigments. It has poor resistance to heat, grease, oil, turpentine, and mineral spirits. Lacking resilience, it dents easily and becomes pocked with permanent depressions.

Ceramic tile, glazed and unglazed, is made from clay fired in kilns. It is fireproof, stainproof, and waterproof but can crack or shatter under the impact of a dropped heavy object. Since ceramic tile is a good conductor of heat, it is excellent as a floor for radiant heating. This quality also makes it a good conductor of cold, which can be discomforting in northern climates in the winter. But for the same reason, it is popular in tropical regions.

Both concrete and flagstone have conductive properties similar to tile, but concrete is less expensive. Indoors, concrete is used for slab floors in basementless houses. Where there are basements, this material is always used for the floor. Far more handsome than concrete, flagstone is an elegant addition to outdoor patios and indoor entrance halls. Its installation is expensive and demands considerable skill.

Cork, the product of cork shavings and resin binder, makes a resilient, comfortable floor. It is available in different sizes and thicknesses. But cork is neither lasting nor inexpensive. It is easily damaged by oil and grease and becomes brittle if washed too frequently. Cork tile should not be used where foot traffic is heavy.

Rubber tile is another floor material that must be protected against grease, oil, and all solvents if it is to give long service. Other harmful agents are alkaline cleaners, varnish, shellac, and lacquer. Rubber tile is available in solid colors and marble-like patterns.

Vinyl is probably the best resilient floor covering. The fact that it is widely used in department stores, hospitals, and commercial buildings attests to its durability, its resistance to dents, oil, grease, and alkalis, and its easy maintenance. Manufactured in a large variety of colors, patterns, and designs, vinyl does not become hard or brittle with age.

WINDOWS

Properly placed windows are essential for light and ventilation. Picture windows are popular in new construction, particularly in ranch houses. Be sure that your window opens to a pleasant view, not a busy road or your neighbor's terrace. Unless it is a double glazed pane with an insulating pocket of air, a surprising amount of heat can pass through in the summer and out in the winter.

Different styles and types of windows serve some requirements better than others. Where you have an option, windows should be chosen by room needs. A hard-to-reach window over the kitchen sink should be a crank-operated casement (Fig. 6.11). The window can easily be cranked to a 90 degree opening for quick ventilation. But a double hung window is awkward to reach.

Bedroom windows provide light and ventilation, but their shape and size may conflict with the need for privacy and wall space for furniture. Installing windows high enough along two walls of the room will satisfy these needs (Fig. 6.12).

Aluminum and steel windows are widely used, but wooden frames still retain their lead. Unlike metal, wood is a poor conductor of heat and does not allow moisture to condense readily on its surface.

Better quality aluminum is anodized—specially treated to resist pitting and roughness caused by weathering. This process also allows the metal to be coated with baked enamel.

Anodized aluminum storm windows add measurably to house comfort in winter. Like insulation, they pay for themselves in fuel savings in a few years. Bought in combination with screens, storm

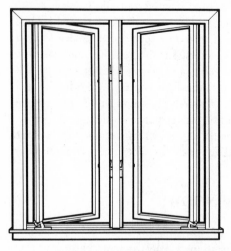

Fig. 6.11
Crank-Operated Casement
Source—Andersen Corporation

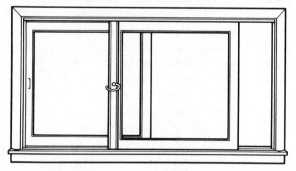

Fig. 6.12   Bedroom Window   *Source—Andersen Corporation*

windows can be raised into the upper sash during summer. In a new dwelling storm windows are always extra. Sometimes a calculating builder will install them on his model house, shrewdly counting on prospects to believe they are getting a good buy. If storm windows are on a model house, ask about them. If you must pay extra for them, allow for their cost in the total purchase price.

Steel windows require more maintenance than other kinds. They must be scraped and painted periodically to prevent rust. Sometimes a steel window is distorted by slamming and other rough use, resulting in serious cold air seepage.

Windows in an older home should operate with ease. Open and close every one; at the same time notice their condition. Look at wooden frames for signs of decay, and check the seams where frames and wall meet. Any space between them should be caulked with a weather-tight sealant. Many unsuspecting buyers have been saddled with the additional expense of replacing rotted windows.

Weather-stripping windows not protected by storm windows will prevent cold air from entering the house. Metal weather-strips are best, particularly if made of spring bronze or similar corrosion-resistant material. Formed into a ridge, the strip is fitted into narrow grooves cut into the frame. When the window is closed, the springy strip forms an air-tight joint. Weather-stripping is also effective against dust, dirt, and sand. Sometimes felt is added for a tighter fit, but a proper installation of metal alone suffices.

For some years a new type of window (Fig. 6.13) has given excellent service at minimal maintenance. It is a crank-operated casement window that combines the insulating value of wood with the extreme durability of rigid vinyl. Made by extruding thick vinyl over a preservative-impregnated wood core, this sash does not need painting, never swells, warps, pits, or corrodes. A double-wall, insulated glass pane is permanently embedded in an inverted-Y channel, and a band of metal stripping forms a weather-tight joint when the window is closed. Moisture will not condense on the surface of this vinyl-covered wood frame. Rigid vinyl is relatively light in weght but has high impact resistance.

DOORS

When examining a house you should look closely at the front and rear doors. Open and close them a few times to determine how well they fit. Also notice the threshold, which is the separate piece of wood fastened to the floor under the door. It should form a weather-tight fit to keep out drafts and windswept rains. The door frame should be tightly caulked.

Interior doors between rooms also merit inspection. Be sure that they close neatly. As you walk through the rooms, slam the doors behind you; the resulting wall vibrations will give you another hint about the dwelling's solidity.

Fig. 6.13
Perma-Shield ™ Window   *Source—Andersen Corporation*

TERMITE PREVENTION

Termites, wood-destroying insects, inhabit every section of the United States, but are most common throughout the eastern half and along the Pacific coast. Feeding on the cellulose in wood, termites cause millions of dollars in damage to homes yearly. Subterranean termites have existed for millions of years, living in the moist soil to which they must return about every twenty-four hours. When exposed to dry air and sunlight, they perish quickly. The damp earth around heated basements and under warm concrete slabs is ideal for nesting termite colonies.

Once termites attack a structure, they proceed to eat their way through all wooden objects within reach—posts, beams, sills, and floors. Since they eat along the grain, causing galleries beneath the surface, termites often remain undetected until the undermined floor or other object is accidentally broken. Access to the structure is gained through wood in contact with the soil, or by way of mud channels which they build up along concrete walls to reach wood.

In late spring, termite kings and queens swarm out of their nests to begin new colonies. They are characterized by dark, straight bodies and long, membranous wings. Unlike flying ants, for which they sometimes are mistaken, termites lack the characteristic pinched waist of the ant; they are uniform in width and about half an inch long. Only mating termites appear in the open, and they nest just long enough to shed their wings, mate, then return to the soil to establish a new colony. Their presence is usually indicated by discarded wings and insects crawling about the window sills, or near doors or cracks in the foundation.

The discovery of shed wings does not invariably mean that termites have begun to attack the woodwork, but it should be construed as a warning. The most likely place to probe for these insects is the basement, where wood is either in actual contact with the ground or separated from it by several inches of concrete.

Since termites destroy wood from the inside, its surface may appear in excellent condition. Stab the suspected wood with a sharp instrument, such as an awl or icepick. If it pierces easily, you may be certain the woodwork is infested with termites. Earthen channels on masonry walls also reveal termites. Breaking the tubes will end activity for that particular group of termites. But fully safeguarding the dwelling calls for more thorough measures.

Termites are tiny enough to pass through cracks no wider than one thirty-second of an inch. A metal shield of copper or zinc installed between the foundation and wooden sill will help to prevent termite infestation. Properly sealed at the joints and projecting downward at least 3 inches from either side at a 45° angle, the shield should have a 2-inch clearance between it and any other object.

Soil that is properly saturated with chlordane or dieldrin will prevent termites from entering the house for ten years or longer. A reputable exterminating firm guarantees its work for a certain number of years, and, if necessary, its workmen will return periodically to inspect the premises and apply more poison. For the do-it-yourself home owner, termite poison is available with full instructions for its proper use. Chlordane and dieldrin are non-toxic to plant life.

Chapter 7

Electricity

Many older houses are not adequately wired, and new ones usually have only minimum wiring. When buying a new house the additional cost of adequate wiring over minimum wiring is between 1 percent and 2 percent of the original price—a small investment that yields excellent dividends. Any extra wiring, switches, and outlets added after the house is completed will be double the cost of the original installation for the same conveniences.

An older home with a 3-wire 120/240 volt service entrance is more valuable than one with a 2-wire 120 volt service. Few houses ten or more years old have been rewired to handle efficiently the multiple appliances and lighting systems used by the average family. Adequate wiring is safer and more economical. A clothes dryer operating on a 3-wire system will use about half the amount of electricity it would on a 2-wire system.

Adequate wiring also means conveniently located outlets, so that lamps and appliances can be used without the awkward tangle of extension cords. With proper wiring, lights burn brighter, irons and toasters heat rapidly, TV screens are clearer, and motor-operated appliances use full power and last longer. More important, the hazard of hot overloaded wires is safely diminished. Wall switches should be located to allow you to enter the house from the front, rear, or side door and walk through every room on all levels from basement to attic without being in the dark, or having to grope for switches, yet not leaving any light on behind you.

Every time a wire is overheated, its insulation softens and then becomes more brittle. In time this protective covering is laced with cracks, exposing the wire. A bare, red hot wire in a wall circuit will easily set fire to any wood it touches. If such a wire in an appliance or power tool contacts the metal housing, the operator may be severely shocked or electrocuted, especially if he is standing on a damp floor.

ELECTRIC CURRENT

Copper is measured in pounds, grain in bushels, and water in gallons. But electricity consists of invisible electrons in constant motion. Water is the closest element to which it can be approximately equated in measurement. The amount or volume of water flowing through a pipe is expressed in gallons per minute. Similarly, the quantity of current flowing along a wire is measured in amperes.

Electricity, like water, can be driven under pressure, and this speed is expressed in volts. Always under pressure, power enters homes at voltages of 120 and 240. In some localities voltages are 115 and 230. A 3-wire system permits the combined use of 120/240 volts. Transmitting electricity along high power lines requires pressures ranging from 2,500 volts for short spans to more than 400,000 volts for long distances.

Wattage is the amount of current that flows past a given point, and refers to the power used. One watt of electricity is the result of one ampere of current propelled by one volt through a circuit. If this flow continues for one hour, one watt-hour of power has been used. Because a watt-hour is a comparatively small unit of energy, it is measured in 1,000-watt units or kilowatts. If a radio rated at 100 watts plays for 10 hours, it will have used one kilowatt.

Most home appliances are rated in watts. More powerful motors are usually rated in amperes, but heavier ones, including those designed for commercial use, are rated in horsepower—another unit of measurement. One horsepower equals 746 watts. Because some power is dissipated as heat, more current is needed to operate a motor. In practical use, one horsepower consumes about 1,000 watts. Smaller motors are often rated in fractional horsepower.

Electricity is generated in both alternating current (AC) and direct current (DC). Only alternating current can be transmitted great distances. It is used in most city and suburban homes. As the current leaves the generating plant, its pressure is stepped up by a transformer to high voltage lines which carry it across the countryside. At cities and towns another type of transformer steps-down the voltage for industrial and commercial use. Current for home use is stepped-down further by secondary transformers.

Because metals vary in resistance to the flow of current, selection of wire material is important. Silver is the best conductor of electricity but its cost is prohibitive. Copper, the next best material, is most commonly used. Less expensive aluminum wire is occasionally used, but it must be thicker than copper to carry the same quantity of electricity.

All current flowing through a wire generates heat. As the quantity increases the wire becomes hotter. If amperage is doubled in the same wire heat is increased fourfold, resulting in wasted energy. Power loss is prevented by increasing the diameter of the wire. No provision can be made for an efficient electric system without considering the thickness or gauge of wires.

Copper conductors or wires are numbered to indicate their maximum amperage. The larger the size number, the smaller the diameter of the wire. The smallest gauge permitted for home wiring is no. 14. The next larger size, no. 12, is recommended for all new wiring. Heavier wires, such as no. 10 and no. 8, are used for major appliances, including clothes dryers and ranges.

CODES

The accepted rules which govern the safe installation of wiring are established by the National Electrical Code, sponsored by the National Fire Protection Association under the auspices of the United States of America Standards Institute. Basic minimum provisions that the Code considers mandatory for safety will assure an installation essentially free from fire hazard.

Underwriters' Laboratories (UL) is a national organization sponsored by manufacturers of electric equipment, insurance companies, and related industries. It tests all kinds of electric devices and wiring materials to determine whether they meet minimum standards of safety and quality. All products tested by UL will carry their label or stamp. Never buy electrical equipment unless it is approved by Underwriters' Laboratories.

While standards and requirements of both Code and Under-writers' are not legally enforceable, states, counties, and cities have enacted laws which ban the use of equipment and materials not approved by UL, and not installed according to the Code. In many localities the Code is augmented by vigorous ordinances. Utility companies will usually refuse to furnish electric power to buildings that are not wired with UL approved materials and installed in conformity with the Code. Nor will insurance companies issue fire policies on such structures.

THE SERVICE ENTRANCE

All wiring from the power company's line to the location inside the house where branch circuits begin comprise the service entrance (Fig. 7.1). The power company supplies the meter and sometimes fur-

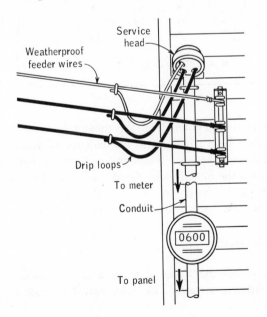

Service head

Weatherproof feeder wires

Drip loops

To meter

Conduit

0600

To panel

Fig. 7.1
3-Wire Electric
Service Entrance

nishes all outside lines leading to it. House lead-in wires may be enclosed in rigid or thin wall conduit, or non-metallic sheathed cable. Whichever is used depends on local requirements. In most localities non-metallic cable is permitted but conduit, or galvanized steel pipe encasing the wires, is preferable. Conduit is more expensive but gives better protection.

The gauge of the wire in the lead-in service installation determines the amount of electricity in the house. The recommended minimum is a 3-wire service with 120/240 volts for 100 amperes to provide 24,000 watts. In new homes the trend is toward 150 or 200 amperes. The Code requires these 3-wire lines to be at least 10 feet above sidewalks and 18 feet over driveways. Meters (Fig. 7.2) are often installed on outside walls for easy access by metermen.

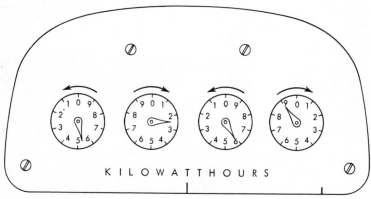

Fig. 7.2   Electric Meter

All electric current used is registered on the meter's four dials in kilowatt hours. Reading from left to right, the dials record 5,269 kilowatt hours. The difference between this figure and the previous month's reading represents the quantity of current used. If a pointer is between two numbers, the lesser one is used. A newer meter is designed like a car's mileage gauge and read with the same case.

Service Entrance Switch

All electric current enters the house through a service panel, then branches off to different circuits. The main switch is located here to let you disconnect the entire wiring system instantly during an emergency or to make repairs.

FUSES, CIRCUITS, AND OUTLETS

Fuses are the safety valves of a home's electric system. A circuit consists of two wires through which current flows from the service entrance panel to one or more outlets and back to the panel. Each circuit is protected against an overload by a fuse, which automatically cuts off power when amperage exceeds the wire's rated capacity. A short alloy strip in the fuse has a lower melting point than that of the wire. In an overloaded circuit the melted strip disconnects the circuit before damage occurs. Blown fuses (Fig. 7.3) are easily identified by their discolored mica windows. A properly designed fuse is the weakest point in a circuit.

Fig. 7.3   Good Fuse   Blown Fuses   *Source—Con Edison*

When a standard plug fuse blows it cannot be used again, a disadvantage in homes with motor-driven appliances. A starting motor requires an extra surge of power for a brief period, and substituting a higher rated fuse is dangerous. Although the motor will continue to operate, the circuit is no longer protected against an overload. Severe damage to the wiring system, even a fire, may result. Equally hazardous is placing a penny, sometimes dubbed an "Abe Lincoln fuse," behind the blown fuse. This practice tops the list of home fires caused by faulty wiring.

Fuses are numbered to indicate their rated amperage. The maximum carrying power of a no. 14 wire circuit under pressure of 120 volts is 15 amperes. No combination of appliances or lights exceeding 1,650 watts should be used on this circuit at any single time. Wattage is the product of volts and amperes: 120 (volts) $\times$ 15 (amperes) = 1,800 watts. A circuit, however, should not be loaded to its full capacity, for a voltage drop impairs the efficiency of lights and appliances. A 20-ampere circuit with no. 12 wire has a maximum capacity of 2,400 watts; however, limiting its use to 2,200 watts provides a margin of safety. Adequate wiring will eliminate the need to place maximum loads on any circuit.

Special plug fuses are made with a time-delay feature to temporarily absorb additional demands for power without damage to the wiring. One type, called *Fusetron,* is available up to 30 amperes, as are other plug fuses. But a short circuit will blow it. *Fustat* is another type that will stand short-time overloads. It has a tamper-proof base to fit a special adaptor. Once the latter is locked into the fuse socket, it cannot be removed. Designed with an off-size base, no higher rated fuse can be inserted. This type too cannot be reused if blown by a short circuit.

The circuit breaker panel is commonly installed in newer houses and those updated with adequate wiring. Serving the same purpose as fuses, circuit breakers have bi-metallic strips that expand at uneven rates. If they are heated above a preset temperature, they curve away and disconnect the circuit. When the breaker is reset manually, the circuit closes, resuming the flow of current. Breakers are designed to take brief overloads without tripping. Short circuits will also open the switch, but it can be reset immediately after the defect causing the short circuit is corrected.

Three types of circuits are recommended by the Code, each intended for definite uses. General purpose circuits are designed to provide outlets throughout the house for lighting and small appliances, except in kitchen, dining, and laundry areas. At least one circuit for each 375 square feet of usable floor area is recommended. Not more than ten outlets should be on a circuit; preferably fewer.

Convenience outlets should be spaced so that no lamp or appliance is more than six feet from an outlet. Locate the outlets about two feet from the end of walls, instead of the center, to allow them to be reached easily without moving bulky furniture. In a well-planned wiring system, all outlets on one floor are not on the same circuit. This prevents a blown fuse from putting the entire floor in darkness.

General purpose circuit wires are usually no. 14 with 15-ampere fuses. Special purpose circuits are 20-ampere appliance circuits for kitchen, dining room, and laundry. At least two circuits are required, independent of lighting fixtures in the kitchen and laundry. Three such circuits will provide an extra margin for future needs.

Convenience outlets in the kitchen should be installed for every four feet of work-counter space. Separate appliance circuits provide an individual circuit for each heavy appliance operating on 20, 30, and higher amperage. Separate circuits are recommended for TV sets, oil burner units, air conditioners, and refrigerators.

To determine how many lights and appliances can be safely plugged into a given circuit at the same time, add their wattage. Each appliance has a name-plate which gives basic facts about its rated capacity, and the conditions under which it will operate most efficiently. An automatic toaster, for example, listed at "1200 watts. 120 volts. AC only," plugged into a 15-ampere circuit leaves a 450 watt margin of safety.

If the toaster is used on a circuit of less than 120 volts, it will draw full current but heat much slower than usual. Plugged into a higher voltage circuit, the appliance will burn out. Since alternating current is used in most homes and farms, there is little likelihood the toaster will be plugged into a direct current line. If the name-plate on a motor-driven appliance does not list the current required, the unit may be powered with a universal motor that operates on either AC or DC.

Shockproof safety outlets are an additional safeguard in homes with young children. Curious youngsters have shocked or electrocuted themselves by inserting nails, wire, and other metal objects into conventional outlets in lower walls. Some homes have outlets placed between 30 and 36 inches above the floor, instead of the usual 12 to 18 inches. This placement serves a twofold function: adults need not bend down or crouch to plug in a cord, and the outlets are out of reach of curious toddlers.

Be sure you have enough electrical outlets to accommodate the TV, radios, air-conditioner, electric blankets, vacuum cleaners, toasters, shavers, heaters, lamps, toothbrushes, sun lamps, washers, dryers, and your never-ending addition of appliances.

SWITCHES AND SAFETY

Wall switches are most conveniently located on the latch side of doors, between 40 and 48 inches from the floor line. The main light source in a room should be switch-controlled. If a room has two entrances, a 3-way switch at either door will control the light from both ends. The light can be turned on when entering and turned off when leaving, without retracing steps. An excellent accident preventive, the 3-way switch decreases the danger of falling over toys and other objects strewn about the floor. This type of switch should also be at the foot and head of every stairway.

All bathroom light switches should be installed at the entrance door, where they cannot be touched by anyone in the bathtub or shower stall. If the light is operated by a pull chain, replace it with an insulated pull cord. Switches and cover plates should be made of insulated material. Electric heaters for a bathroom are safest when they are recessed in the wall.

APPLIANCE WATTAGE TABLE

In estimating the amount of electricity required use Table 2, which lists appliances and their average wattage. Figures vary because manufacturers produce the same appliances with differently rated capacities.

LIGHTING

Two types of lighting are used in the average home—general lighting for all areas and local lighting for reading, writing, and other specific jobs. More light is given by one high watt bulb than several smaller ones that have the same total wattage. A single 100-watt bulb, for example, emits more light than four 25-watt bulbs. Bulbs blackened from use give less light at higher cost per watt and should be discarded.

Contrast in lighting is a chief cause of eyestrain. A bright television screen in an otherwise dark room acts as a spotlight on the eyes, compelling them to continually shift from brightness to dark-

TABLE 2

TYPICAL WATTAGE · DOMESTIC APPLIANCES

	WATTS		WATTS
Air Conditioners—Room		Heat Lamp	250
Coolers ...... up to	2700	Heating Pad	60
Aquarium Equipment ...	150	Hi-Fi Equipment	230
Blanket	190	Hot Plate .... up to	1650
Blender	275	Humidifier	50
Bottle Warmer	500	Ice Cream Freezer	115
Broiler	1500	Iron—Dry or Steam	1000
Casserole	1150	Ironer	1580
Chafing Dish	1150	Knife Sharpener	40
Clock	2	Power Tools ..... up to	1000
Clothes Dryer		Pressure Cooker	1300
Electric—Conventional	5600	Projector .... up to	1280
Electric—High Speed ..	8400	Radio	30
Gas	400	Ranges	
Clothes Washer	400	Free Standing up to	16000
Clothes—Washer—Dryer	6000	Wall Ovens .. up to	8000
Coffee Maker .... up to	1000	Built-in Cooking Tops	
Corn Popper	600	up to	8200
Dehumidifier	190	Recorder	60
Deodorizer ...... up to	360	Record Player	75
Dishwasher	1400	Refrigerator	320
Door Chime	15	Roaster	1320
Egg Cooker	1100	Sandwich Grill ... up to	1300
Fans		Sewing Machine	75
Window	210	Shaver	11
Attic	400	Sun Lamp	275
Kitchen Exhaust	55	Tea Kettle ...... up to	1000
Portable	160	Toaster	1200
Floor Polisher	400	TV Receiver—Black and	
Food Freezer .... up to	425	White	205
Food Mixer	150	TV Receiver—Color	420
Food Warmer .... up to	1000	Vacuum Cleaners	
Fry Kettle	1320	Bag .... up to	550
Frying Pan	1150	Canister—Tank up to	1000
Hair Dryer	330	Hand	155
Heater .... up to	1650	Vaporizer	350
Heating Equipment		Waffle Baker ..... up to	1300
Furnace Fan	320	Water Heater .. up to	10000
Oil Burner Motor up to	550		

Source—Con Edison

ness. An indirect lamp, with its light diffused against a white ceiling, will diminish the disparity. Whenever the quantity of light is intensified for a specific visual task, the contrast should be reduced by increasing the general light.

Glare is unshielded or unshaded light that strikes the eyes. Direct glare emanates from a bright light source. Indirect glare is caused by reflected light from a smooth surface such as glossy paper or a glass desk top. Glare occurs while the eyes adapt to different light situations.

Good quality lighting is diffused to help prevent glare. By spreading light rays in all directions, the entire surface reflects soft light. Plastic and translucent glass shades are intended to diffuse light. A well-designed shade is dense enough to prevent the bulb from shining through as a ball of light, but allows softly diffused light for comfortable use. Bulbs are frosted on the inside to reduce glare.

Incandescent bulbs and fluorescent tubes are the two sources of light in the home. An incandescent bulb has a filament of hair-thin tungsten wire which glows white hot when electricity passes through it.

Fluorescent lighting, introduced in 1939, gives more than three times as much light per watt of electricity than incandescent bulbs. While the latter will burn from 750 to 1,000 hours, most fluorescent tubes will last well beyond 7,500 hours. The burning life of a tube is reduced when it is switched on and off too often. It is more economical to leave the light on for short periods rather than turn it off.

Designed in straight or circular tubes, fluorescent lighting is not produced by electricity flowing through a filament. The sealed tube contains small amounts of mercury and argon gas, and the inner surface is coated with fluorescent substances called phosphors. At each end is an electrode. An electric current converts the mercury vapor to invisible violet light that causes the phosphor coating to fluoresce or glow. By varying the amounts of phosphors, several tones of white light are produced. Since they emit much cooler light than incandescent bulbs, fluorescent lamps are especially desirable in confined areas.

Sometimes if fluorescent lamps interfere with radio reception, plugging either the radio or lamp into an outlet on a different circuit will eliminate the noise. Shifting these units farther from each other is also effective. Installing radio interference filters at the radio or in the service entrance panel, where fluorescent lamp circuits branch, will also reduce much of the static.

Structural Lighting

Home light sources permanently fixed to the ceilings and walls are described as structural lighting. This term applies to installations devised to fit a specific purpose. Custom-built into walls and ceilings, structural lighting can blend with any color scheme or decorating motif, and its usually minimal styling does not give a dated appearance.

Since walls and ceilings represent 75 percent or more of room surface in the house, structural lighting accentuates these areas. Proper wall lighting creates the illusion of receding walls and increases the room's apparent size. Almost all structural lighting is designed for fluorescent lamps.

Structural lighting techniques are mostly of the general type, but in a few instances they are used for local lighting. Valance lights are invariably placed over windows below the ceiling, and their light is reflected downward from the ceiling on the draperies. If placed nearer than ten inches to a white ceiling, the top of the valance should be covered or closed to prevent ceiling glare.

Structural lighting installed in cornices can be used to highlight murals, wall coverings, and draperies or, if mounted at the junction of wall and ceiling, can accentuate the walls and create an impression of greater ceiling height. Cornice lights are used most advantageously in low-ceilinged rooms, especially recreation areas and basements.

Cove lighting is best suited to rooms with high ceilings, because all its light is directed toward the ceiling. If considerable light is to be reflected downward into the room, the ceiling should be white or near-white. If the cove is made of a luminous or translucent panel, the lighting is softly diffused. Although cove lighting provides good background light for watching television, it is inadequate for general lighting when used alone and should be supplemented with other lighting.

Wall brackets can be used on almost any windowless wall in the house. High wall brackets afford good general lighting; vertical light is directed both up and down, thus shielding the eyes. Low

TABLE 3

LAMP SELECTION GUIDE

INCANDESCENT   HIGH INTENSITY DISCHARGE LAMPS

Lamp Names	Filament **	Clear Mercury	White Mercury	Deluxe White * Mercury	Multi-Vapor *	Lucalox **
Efficacy (Lumens/watt)	Low	Medium	Medium	Medium	High	High
Lamp appearance effect on neutral surfaces	Yellowish white	Greenish blue-white	Greenish white	Purplish white	Greenish white	Yellowish
Effect on "atmosphere"	Warm	Very cool, Greenish	Moderately cool, Greenish	Warm, Purplish	Moderately cool, Greenish	Warm, Yellowish
Colors strengthened	Red Orange Yellow	Yellow Green Blue	Yellow Green Blue	Red Yellow Blue	Yellow Green Blue	Yellow Orange Green
Colors greyed	Blue	Red, Orange	Red, Orange	Green	Red	Red, Blue
Effect on complexions	Ruddiest	Greenish	Very pale	Ruddy	Greyed	Yellowish
Remarks	Good color rendering	Very poor color rendering	Moderate color rendering	Color acceptance similar to CW fluorescent	Color acceptance similar to CW fluorescent	Color acceptance approaches that of WW fluorescent

Source—General Electric

98

FLUORESCENT LAMPS

Lamp Names	Cool * White	Deluxe * Cool White	Warm ** White	Deluxe ** Warm White	Daylight	White	Soft White/ Natural
Efficacy (Lumens/ watt)	High	Medium	High	Medium	Medium-High	High	Medium
Lamp appearance effect on neutral surfaces	White	White	Yellowish white	Yellowish white	Bluish white	Pale yellowish white	Purplish white
Effect on "atmosphere"	Neutral to moderately cool	Neutral to moderately cool	Warm	Warm	Very Cool	Moderately warm	Warm pinkish
Colors strengthened	Orange, Yellow, Blue	All nearly equal	Orange, Yellow	Red, Orange, Yellow, Green	Green, Blue	Orange, Yellow	Red, Orange
Colors greyed	Red	None appreciably	Red, Green Blue	Blue	Red, Orange	Red, Green, Blue	Green, Blue
Effect on complexions	Pale Pink	Most natural	Sallow	Ruddy	Greyed	Pale	Ruddy Pink
Remarks	Blends with natural daylight— Good color acceptance	Best overall color rendition; simulates natural daylight	Blends with incandescent light—poor color acceptance	Good color rendition; simulates incandescent light	Usually replaceable with CW	Usually replaceable with CW or WW	Tinted Source Usually replaceable with CWX or WWX

* Greater preference at higher levels. ** Greater preference at lower levels.

99

brackets are working lights intended for uses close to the wall—over desks, sofas, and beds. These should be placed no higher than 5 feet from the floor.

Fluorescent and incandescent light impart color qualities ranging from warm to very cool. Visually pleasing light tones are largely a matter of personal preference. Table 3 is an overall guide for lamp selection according to color effects on people, surroundings, and objects.

Chapter 8

Plumbing

WATER SUPPLY

The plumbing system begins where fresh water enters the main house line under pressure (as it does if it is supplied by a municipal system) and ends where waste water and material leave through the drainage line. Piped in at about 40 PSI (pounds per square inch) pressure, water has enough force to rise to a second and even a third floor if the pipes are large enough. If water pressure in the area tends to be spasmodically low, the lead-in main should be one inch in diameter.

The main shut-off valve is properly located at the inside wall where the water line enters the dwelling. In case of an emergency, such as a broken pipe, the valve will enable you to shut off the water supply to the house. This protective device is also essential when the water system in an unoccupied and unheated home must be drained during freezing weather.

Galvanized metal pipe was previously used for plumbing. It is zinc-coated iron or steel. Once the protective layer of zinc wears away, the metal underneath begins to corrode until the pipe is choked with rust. A reduced flow of water is the first symptom. Soon the wall of the pipe is gnawed through, resulting in serious leakage. Now brass pipe and copper tubing have largely replaced galvanized iron pipe. Properly installed and used, these will last as long as the house.

101

To test the water supply, turn on the faucets in the wash basin and tub and, at the same time, flush the toilet. If the water flow is reduced to a dribble, the most likely cause is rust-clogged galvanized pipes. Visually identifying brass or copper is not easy if the pipes have been in use for some years, because the outer surface oxidizes with age. Scraping a small area slightly with a pocket knife will reveal the characteristically yellow-red luster of brass; copper will be distinctly reddish in color. A small magnet is another useful testing device; it will cling to ferrous metal, such as iron or steel, but not to brass or copper.

Without valves at every fixture to shut off the water supply, the entire house must be deprived of water whenever local plumbing repairs, such as changing a washer in a faucet, are made. These shut-off valves should be located behind every sink, tub, and toilet.

In a sensibly designed system hot and cold water pipes are not too close together; otherwise only tepid water will flow from the cold water faucet. Mixed plumbing of this type is expensive to rearrange correctly. All cold water lines should be to your right on the fixture.

The common causes of noisy plumbing are water supply and drain pipes which are freestanding, that is, not fastened to structural members in the wall. Running water vibrates such loose lines, causing an irksome chatter. This problem, which appears only in two-level houses, can be solved effectively by making one or two six-inch openings in the wall, vertically in line with the pipes, and then cushioning the pipes in sound absorbent insulation.

Another plumbing noise is the ringing bang that occurs when water is shut off abruptly, rattling the pipes and echoing throughout the house. It is caused by the impetus of pressure-driven water, which is incompressible, slamming into the closed valve. This noise is diminished when pipes are rigidly fastened to structural members in the walls and can be altogether eliminated by an air chamber device fastened to the pipe near the faucet. Instead of hammering against the closed valve, the water's force is cushioned against an air pocket in the device.

Hot Water

Hot water lines are not intended to act as heating units for the house, but any uninsulated surface functions as a radiator, and bare hot water lines lose about 20 percent of their heat. Good insulation, which is fireproof and a very poor conductor of heat, will assure more uniform and satisfactory water temperature throughout the year. Pipe insulation is available in sleeves designed to fit lines of any size.

PLUMBING FIXTURES

Sinks, tubs, and other plumbing fixtures are made in a wide range of varying quality. Low priced bathtubs in lightweight steel are finished with material that becomes rough and discolors quickly. A continual drip of water will wear away the thin enamel coat, exposing the iron to rust. Cast iron tubs, encased in a heavy layer of baked enamel, are preferable. Wash basins and sinks made of vitreous china will retain their appearance much better than a cast iron unit with an enamel surface.

All water closets or toilets are made of vitreous china. A good bowl has a water area with a wide outflow passage to prevent obstruction, self-cleaning facilities, and quiet, whirlpool-like flushing action. The siphon-jet bowl most closely meets these requirements. Oval-like in form, it is easiest to clean, most efficient, and most expensive. Second to this is the reverse-trap bowl which costs half as much as the siphon-jet. The least expensive is the wash-down type of bowl. Containing less than half the water surface of the siphon-jet, it is not self-cleaning or easy to clean and is noisy when flushed. Its relatively narrow outflow passage may become obstructed by objects that could easily pass through the siphon-jet and reverse-trap models.

SEWAGE DISPOSAL SYSTEMS

Public Sewerage Facilities

Where public sewers are available, the municipality provides sewer trunk lines in the streets and connections from trunk line to the curb for each house. Installing the connecting line from house to curb is the home owner's responsibility. Assessment for the main trunk line and sewage disposal plant is apportioned among the home owners. Since it is not unusual for several years to elapse before the assessment charges are levied, you should ascertain whether the seller of a house you are considering paid for his sewer installation.

In the absence of public sewerage facilities, a tract developer may install a private disposal system for homes in the subdivision. Sewer lines are provided from homes to streets and then converge to the private disposal facility, which often is a massive septic tank system. This kind of facility saves the home owner future costs of connecting from a separate private system when public sewers become available, because the already installed pipes are connected to the public sewage facility without need to dig up streets and lawns.

Some local planning boards require tract developers to post bonds or file liability insurance policies assuring the installation and proper maintenance of sewage disposal facilities. Bonds also guarantee the builder will complete other off-site work, such as curbs, paved streets, and catch basins for rain water. When inspecting homes in a new development, visit the municipal center or borough hall, where you can read a copy of the resolution and contract that spell out in detail the builder's obligations. If paved streets are not included, you may live in a sea of mud for a long time, besides being assessed for the local improvement when they are paved.

Blockage of sewer lines by tree roots between house and curb is a common nuisance, more likely to occur in clay pipes than those of cast iron. Sealed with oakum and lead, cast iron pipe will provide long, trouble-free service. If tree root blockage does occur, the roots in the sewer line will have to be periodically cut—this procedure is known as "roto-rooting."

Cesspools

In areas lacking municipal sewers, homes must rely on a private means of waste disposal, either by cesspool or septic tank. The cesspool is a large hole in the ground lined with curved, perforated concrete blocks laid without mortar for easy drainage. Raw sewage from the house drain is discharged directly into the cesspool.

Liquid waste drained into the cesspool is absorbed by the soil, and bacteria in the waste decompose the solids. Powerful bleaches and detergents in large quantities retard the action of these organisms. In time the cesspool wall becomes coated with grease from the kitchen sink, forcing the liquid waste to back up into the house. Where there are cesspools, it is a prudent practice to drain off cooking fats into containers for disposal with other kitchen refuse rather than washing them down the sink.

Cesspools are unsatisfactory in dense clay or marshy ground. Even in sandy or porous earth, heavy rains may saturate the soil, preventing the cesspool's contents from leaching into the ground. At other times the cesspool may overflow because too much water drains into it at one time. Chemical compounds are sold with the claim that they will eliminate clogged cesspools or septic tanks; however, most of these products do not live up to their promise.

There are firms that specialize in cleaning cesspools. After most of the contents have been pumped out, five or more gallons of sulphuric acid are poured into the remaining liquid. This combination generates an intensely hot solution that dissolves grease adhering to the wall.

Sometimes, digging a new cesspool next to the faulty one offers a better solution. The old one then becomes a trap to prevent grease from flowing into the new cesspool. But a well-designed septic tank is preferable.

Cesspools that are replaced by public sewer facilities should be cleaned and disinfected, then filled with dirt or sand. With the passage of time their mortarless walls weaken and sometimes collapse when people stand or children play over them.

Septic Tanks

The septic tank is a hygienic method for disposing of waste matter. It is a watertight and airtight unit, made of either masonry or steel, that holds waste matter until it is liquefied by bacterial action. A residue of insoluble sludge sinks to the bottom and the liquid drains along several rows of clay disposal pipes where it seeps through the loosely fitted joints into the soil. The sludge must be cleaned out periodically.

FHA minimum standards for septic tanks vary with the size of the family. A three-bedroom house with a maximum of six occupants, for example, requires a tank with a 900 gallon capacity. In dwellings with five or more bedrooms, the tank capacity should be at least 1,250 gallons.

Like cesspools, septic tanks will not function properly in clayish or boggy soil, nor if large amounts of grease and detergents are discharged into them. Chemicals that allegedly improve bacterial action are no substitute for periodic inspection and cleaning. In most areas where this type of waste disposal is used, there are firms that will contract to inspect and clean your septic tank periodically. Although yearly inspections are recommended, many large families have learned from distressing experience that even a large capacity tank can back up much sooner. A dry well for run-off water from the washing machine will help prevent serious backflow problems.

Be sure you learn the exact location of the cesspool or septic tank from the seller or builder, because digging blindly for one on a large plot can be a very costly procedure.

Chapter 9

Insulation, Heating, and Air-Conditioning

INSULATION

Insulation serves to keep a house warmer in winter and cooler in summer. Most types of insulation also tend to reduce noise. Inorganic insulating material such as mineral wool or fiberglass is fire retardant and rat-proof and cannot be eaten by insects. A well-insulated home adds greatly to comfort and represents substantial savings in fuel. In northern areas subject to harsh winters, good insulation will actually pay for itself in fuel savings in a few years.

Whenever people, particularly the very young and old, have difficulty adjusting to sharply varying temperatures, they are likely to suffer colds. Older houses with ill-fitting windows and doors are a major cause of colds. Too many chilling drafts enter and too much heat is lost. Insulation prevents this.

Many early American builders understood the value of insulation. Wall spaces in their large, drafty houses were filled with sawdust, wood shavings, or seaweed.

Heat is transferred in three different ways: by conduction, convection, or radiation. Conduction is the transmittal of heat through a solid object, such as the handle of a pot of boiling water; convection is the movement of heated air from warm to cold zones; and radia-

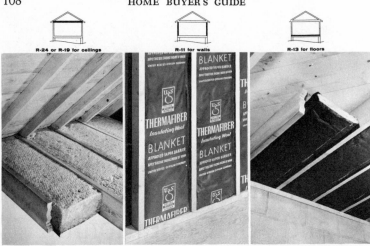

Fig. 9.1   Insulation   *Source—United States Gypsum Company*

tion is heat energy that flows through air to cold surfaces, such as the sun's rays passing through the atmosphere to the earth. Insulation is designed to prevent heat loss through a wall by any of these means in the winter, and to keep heat out of the house in the summer.

Modern insulation was introduced in about 1950. Prewar houses are without this type of insulation protection unless the owners have added it since then. Insulation is most effective when installed in a house under construction (Fig. 9.1), but much can be done in one that has already been built. The material can be put in an unfinished attic or under the floor of an unheated crawl space, and blown into the space between exterior and interior walls. Small openings are made in the exterior walls, allowing granules or pellets to be blown in by air pressure.

Two general types of insulation are: the poor heat conductors and the good heat reflectors. Included among the former are fiberglass, mineral wool, vermiculite, asbestos, and gypsum. These are made in flexible batts, blankets, rigid panels, or loose fill. Their low heat conducting properties are due to countless minute pockets in which the trapped air cannot flow and cause heat loss by convection. Reflective insulation has a bright metallic surface such as aluminum foil, which reflects the radiated heat back into the house, just as a mirror reflects radiated light.

Besides having poor conducting properties, insulation should be fireproof. The use of combustible material between walls is extremely hazardous. Inorganic insulating material will reduce the danger of fire.

Because the sole purpose of insulation is to resist the passage of heat in any direction—from leaving the house in winter and from entering it in the summer—the tested resistance (R) is based on all the influencing factors of conductivity, density, thickness, and installed location. Insulation manufactured to these specifications will be marked by the R number. The higher the number, the greater the resistance to heat flow. Thus a batt marked R-19 will provide better insulation than one with an R-11.

Since glass has very low insulating value, much heat is lost through the windows. This is uncomfortably evident in cold weather when house moisture turns to frost on contact with windows. It is helpful to weather-strip windows and caulk loose joints around the frames; but these measures are no substitute for properly installed aluminum storm windows and doors, which form an almost airtight space that prevents heat loss through conduction. Double-glazed windows serve the same purpose.

Condensation is a winter problem. Warm air has a larger capacity for moisture than cold air before it condenses into droplets. When indoor humidity becomes excessive, condensation occurs, appearing first as droplets or frost on uninsulated windows. If allowed to increase, moisture will condense on uninsulated walls facing the outside, causing the continually wet wood to rot. It will also wet through and weaken plaster and blister the exterior paint. Vapor barriers between the inner and exterior walls will prevent this condition.

A vapor barrier (Fig. 9.2) may be a moisture-proof cover, such as aluminum foil, on insulating batts or blankets. Sometimes it is a polyethylene plastic membrane which covers the inner side of the exterior wall. To be effective, the vapor barrier must separate the insulation from the interior of the dwelling. A waterproof membrane is also necessary under the concrete floor of a house built on a slab.

Excessive humidity can easily be avoided. It is caused by water vapor from cooking, bathing, washing and drying clothes, or humidifiers. Outside causes may be roof leaks or faulty construction around doors and windows causing low resistance to driving rains that result in leaks. Other faults may be seepage in the foundation, or lack of insulation and vapor barriers under crawl spaces. Ventilation can prevent much of this discomfort. Exhaust fans in the kitchen

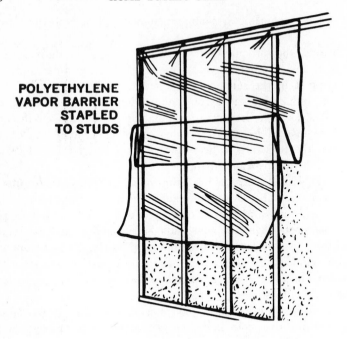

POLYETHYLENE VAPOR BARRIER STAPLED TO STUDS

Fig. 9.2 Vapor Barrier *Source—United States Gypsum Company*

and bathroom as well as a vented laundry dryer will noticeably reduce humidity. Warm-air heating systems tend to hold the humidity level low. Sometimes comfort demands that this level be raised by a humidifier.

HEATING SYSTEMS

Most people are comfortable at temperatures ranging from 68° to 75° with humidity between 45 percent to 55 percent. If the thermostat is set at 72° but the temperature does not rise to this level despite a constantly operating boiler, the cause is either an inadequate heating system, an uninsulated house, or both.

The main systems of modern central heating are forced warm air, steam, hot water or hydronic, electric, and radiant heat. When properly installed, each provides adequate heat.

Steam heat is produced in a boiler and rises through pipes into

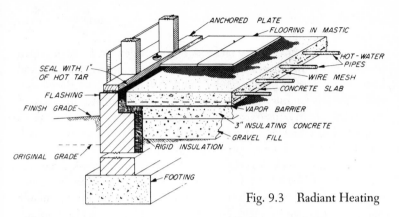

Fig. 9.3   Radiant Heating

radiators. After the steam yields its heat, it condenses to water and returns through the same pipe to the boiler for reheating. This is called the one-pipe system. The two-pipe system provides for the steam to rise in one pipe and the water to return in another. In both systems, all radiators must be at higher levels than the boiler. The two-pipe system is more costly and is seldom found in a one-family home. It can readily be recognized by observing whether a radiator has a second pipe leading away from it.

Hydronic or *hot water house heating* is also divided into two systems: gravity and forced circulation. In both systems, the boiler and all pipes and radiators are filled with water. Each radiator has two pipes, one to conduct hot water from the boiler, the other to return the cooled water.

The gravity system functions on the physical law that heated water, like hot air, expands, becomes lighter, and rises, while the cooler water contracts, becomes heavier, and flows down to the boiler.

The forced circulation system is preferable. An electrical pump attached near the boiler thrusts the hot water through the system, heating the house much faster. The higher efficiency allows for a smaller boiler. A cast iron boiler will easily outlast a steel one. It should bear the seal of the Institute of Boiler and Radiator Manufacturers (IBR) on its nameplate. A steel boiler corrodes more quickly, particularly if the local water is hard. The nameplate on a steel boiler which conforms to established standards will show the seal of the Steel Boiler Institute (SBI).

Radiant heat (Fig. 9.3) is produced by hot water coursing through coiled copper tubing (usually installed in a cement floor), or by electrical wires embedded in the ceiling. Radiant heat wall panels are not so efficient.

Radiant heating is the second oldest system devised by man (open fire was first). In ancient Rome, all public buildings and substantial homes had floor panels heated from below by hot air. Because it was relatively simple, this type of heat was also used in parts of Asia during early historical times. More than two thousand years ago, Koreans protected themselves against harsh winters with radiant floor heating—a system they still use today.

Considerable technical knowledge and skill are required for proper installation of hot-water radiant heating. Modern hot-water radiant floor heat is usually found in dwellings built on a concrete slab in which copper pipes are embedded. The pipes must be embedded in the cement slab before the house is built. In larger, substantially built houses, the copper pipes may be installed in ceilings. Wall radiation is suitable in bathrooms and other small spaces, where neither ceiling nor floor area is sufficient for this type of heating. Radiant wall panels in larger rooms are uncomfortably hot when people are too near them.

Aside from providing more uniform heating, radiant heating saves space. But it has disadvantages, such as a sluggish heating time lag and difficult access for repairs. Sometimes draperies and carpeting will adversely affect floor panel systems. For this reason, Europeans show a decided preference for ceiling panels.

Electric heating, which is less expensive to install than other systems, is usually in the form of baseboard units, with each room individually controlled by a thermostat. Heat is produced by a high-resistance wire similar to that in a toaster. But no glow is seen because the wire is covered with high-temperature insulation.

Wires or cables in the ceiling also provide safe radiant heating. Sometimes ceiling heat causes the plaster to lose its cohesive bond and crumble. This can be avoided by preparing plaster to the specifications of either the American Society for Testing Materials or American Standards Association.

Electric heat responds instantly and is cleaner and more efficient than conventional heating systems. It eliminates the need for a boiler, chimney, pipes, ducts, pumps, or other controls. Only thermostats are required. Although maintenance is indeed low, the cost of electric heat is higher than that of gas or oil except in a few areas of the country.

Electric heat cannot be efficient unless the house is fully insulated and has double-pane or aluminum storm windows and doors. A new house equipped with electric heating should therefore be carefully inspected.

Many builders install electric heating because of its low initial cost —but check on the local electricity rates; they may be high. Be sure, too, that the electric heating system conforms to standards of the National Electrical Manufacturers Association (NEMA).

Dry heat may be the gravity type or the more efficient forced warm-air system. Gravity heating is likely to be found in older houses. Conspicuous floor grills or registers, into which dirt and other objects fall easily, typify this kind of heating. Bulky air ducts extend octopus-like from an oversize furnace that prevents the basement from being used for extra living space.

Heat is produced in the furnace which is encased in a heavy metal shell. A fire in the inner chamber heats the air between it and the outer shell. As the hot air expands and becomes lighter in weight, it rises through the large ducts leading to the floor registers. Upon losing its heat, the cooler air becomes heavier, settles to the floor, and flows down the cold-air ducts to the furnace for reheating.

Gravity heating is inefficient and obsolete. No dust-removal filter can be used in this system without slowing and seriously interfering with the air movement. Dust, odors, and sound travel unhindered from one room to another through the metal ducts, which also must be short in length to prevent the slow-moving air from dissipating its heat before reaching the upper floors. For this reason, warm-air registers are located at the inner walls nearest the furnace, which must be placed in the center of the basement. As the air flows down against the colder outside walls to the return duct, it has already yielded most of its heat. This explains why outer walls are uncomfortably chilly in houses heated by gravity warm-air.

Forced warm-air heating (Fig. 9.4.), in wide use today, is similar but superior to the gravity system. An electric blower draws cooled air down the ducts, then forces it through the hot fire chamber and up again to the rooms. Forced warm air is one of the best heating systems today and does not require high differences in temperature to circulate the air. In mild weather the warming air need not be very hot, merely slightly higher than the desired room temperature.

A smaller forced warm-air furnace will produce equal or more

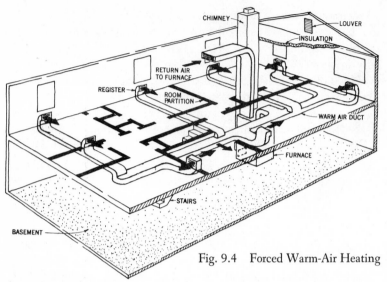

Fig. 9.4   Forced Warm-Air Heating

heat than the gravity type. Moreover, its heating response is rapid; dust-removal filters and humidifiers will contribute to cleanliness and comfort. Since such a furnace need not be located in the center of the basement, this area can be utilized for family activities. Among the system's advantages is its built-in facility for economical air-conditioning.

Zone heating is designed to provide heat to the house area or zone that needs it but not to other sections which are warm enough. Because of shifting winds and changing sunlight, it is virtually impossible to have uniform temperature throughout some houses. In split-level homes, most of the heat rises up the spacious stair passages, resulting in warm upper levels and cool lower floors.

This problem is avoided by dividing the house into zones, with the heat in each controlled by individual thermostats. The lower level can be separately heated, for example, without additional heat going to the already warm upper level. In either case, the zone requiring heat will signal for it through its own thermostat. Flexible and convenient, zone heating can be installed for different levels and separate sections.

Fuel

Gas and oil are the two conventional fuels for boilers and furnaces. Electricity is rarely used in central heating due to its prohibitive cost. Gas heating is slightly more efficient as a fuel than oil, but its rates are higher in most sections of the United States. This type of system is initially less costly than oil. No fuel tank is needed, and maintenance costs are lower. An oil burner will not retain its efficiency unless it is cleaned and serviced yearly. Properly installed and maintained, both systems are equally clean.

Heating Costs

Heating costs of a used home can be determined in several ways. Usually inspecting the seller's heating bills is a fairly accurate guide, provided you know the family's routine. However, low heating bills can be misleading if the family is out during the day, and the thermostat is set at 60° until nightfall. Or a thrifty seller may not heat his upper floors. Nationally known manufacturers of heating equipment will furnish names of reputable local contractors whose estimates are dependable. Some local utility companies will conduct a survey of the home, then guarantee that heating costs will not exceed their estimates.

DOMESTIC WATER HEATING

All modern gas and oil fired boilers are equipped with tankless water heaters. These are coiled copper pipes in which the domestic water is automatically heated. They are designed to assure an ample supply of hot water for today's multi-bathroom houses. But many homes with older, inadequate boilers require domestic water heaters to supplement their hot water supply.

Gas and oil fired water heaters are made in varying degrees of quality—galvanized, aluminum, iron, ceramic or glass lined, or Monel (a durable copper-nickel alloy). A galvanized tank has a short life, and should be avoided whenever possible. Electrically heated units cost more to operate, except in localities where off-peak rates are reasonably moderate. Off-peak time slots are during late nighttime and certain daytime hours when the load demand drops.

Many fortunate home owners in the sub-tropical South and Southwest utilize the sun's abundant rays to heat domestic water with solar energy. A standard 4 x 12 foot solar panel under a blazing sun will provide free hot water endlessly.

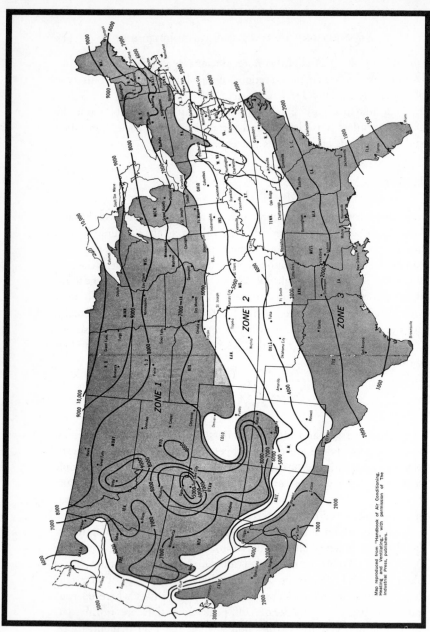

Zone Map
for Heating
and
Air
Conditioning

Fig. 9.5

Zone Map   *Source—National Forest Productions Association*

ZONE MAP FOR HEATING
AND AIR-CONDITIONING

The season's coldness is measured by the number of "degree days," when the temperature falls below 65°F. Each unit is determined by the day's average temperature and subtracted from 65°. For example, a high of 60° and a low of 40° results in an average of 50° (60° + 40° = 100 divided by 2). Subtracting this from 65° shows 15 "degree days" for that day.

In addition to predicting fuel consumption, the degree days in different zones indicate the amount of insulation needed for a home. More insulation should be provided in walls, ceilings, and floors for air-conditioned homes in Zone 2 and 3. Insulation in Zone 1 is satisfactory for air-conditioning.

ZONE 1—Extreme winter, typical winter temperatures range from −10° to 15° F. or colder; degree days: 6000+ Maximum amount of insulation required.

ZONE 2—Intermediate winter weather conditions; temperatures range from 5° to −5° F.; degree days: 3000 to 6000 Moderate insulation required.

ZONE 3—Warm climate; degree days: 500 to 3000 Minimum insulation required.

AIR-CONDITIONING

Each year fewer people consider summer comfortable without some air-conditioning. Common in most office buildings and retail shops, air-conditioning is becoming increasingly popular in homes. Its advantages in providing coolness are self-evident. Cleaner and more comfortable living cuts time spent on housecleaning, and outside noise and humidity are reduced. Controlling the surrounding atmosphere will eventually be as important to residential living as central heating.

Central air-conditioning can be economically adapted to a forced warm-air heating system by a conversion unit. The cooling and dehumidifying coil is attached in the lead-off duct of the furnace, then coupled by two refrigerant pipes to an air-cooled refrigerating unit located directly outside the house. The unit is combined with the furnace dust-removal filter and fan. The house will thus have year-round air-conditioning.

In homes without forced warm-air heating, another type of central air-conditioning can be installed. Gas or oil fired heating is combined with electrical cooling and dehumidifying in a single cabinet. Occupying about three square feet of floor space, this unit will provide air-conditioning throughout the year. Its operation includes removal of dirt, dust, and pollen while circulating purified air through the duct system of the house. Well-made units are quiet enough to be installed even in sleeping areas.

Wet heat systems are not adaptable for central air-conditioning. Homes with steam or hot-water heat can be air-conditioned for hot weather only by the installation of a separate cabinet fitted with a cooling coil, circulating fan, and filter. Such a unit may be located in any unused area—crawl space, attic, or the top of a closet. It can also be joined to a refrigerating device outside the house.

Small units used to air-condition individual rooms include the basic elements for cooling, dehumidifying, filtering, and circulating air. These are intended for windows or an opening in a wall. Larger models are equipped for heating as well. All of these units must be exposed to outside air for condensing the refrigerant.

When contracting for the installation of central air-conditioning, follow suggestions in Chapter 12. Buy only equipment made by nationally known companies who will give you a list of suppliers and contractors in your area. After obtaining three or more estimates of unit capacity, you can make a decision that will minimize risks. Request a performance guarantee that the air-conditioning will provide the comfort promised even on the hottest days; that is, it will keep the temperature to a maximum of 75° F. with a maximum relative humidity of 55 percent. (See Table 4.) Also ask for a warranty against defects in materials and workmanship for a specified period; no reputable contractor should refuse this request.

TABLE 4

1. Determine the wall with maximum outdoor exposure (West Maximum and North Minimum).
2. Which factor exists:
   a. Ceiling under occupied room or insulated ceiling under attic.
   b. Uninsulated ceiling under attic.
3. Size of room: Length x Width (Sq. Feet) is your Key Number.
4. Take your Key Number and find the closest figure to this in the appropriate column determined by following the above steps. The Btu column will indicate the estimated Btus required.

ROOM AIR CONDITIONER SELECTION GUIDE

BTU'S	WEST		SOUTH		EAST		NORTH	
	Ceiling under occupied room or insulated ceiling under attic	Un-insulated ceiling under attic	Ceiling under occupied room or insulated ceiling under attic	Un-insulated ceiling under attic	Ceiling under occupied room or insulated ceiling under attic	Un-insulated ceiling under attic	Ceiling under occupied room or insulated ceiling under attic	Un-insulated ceiling under attic
33,000	1740	1000	1820	1050	1920	1090	2150	1230
27,000	1440	830	1510	870	1590	900	1785	1010
23,000	1140	670	1300	710	1270	730	1420	830
18,000	860	510	920	540	970	560	1060	620
17,000	800	475	870	505	915	525	1005	585
16,000	750	440	820	470	860	490	950	545
15,000	685	405	750	430	790	450	870	500
14,000	620	370	680	390	720	410	790	450
13,000	595	330	605	350	645	365	680	405
12,000	470	285	530	305	570	325	625	355
11,000	442	268	445	265	535	305	555	320
10,000	365	205	360	225	390	235	425	260
8,500	290	180	310	200	355	215	380	235
8,000	230	140	250	160	290	185	330	210
7,500	170	125	220	140	240	160	280	180
6,000	150	100	170	110	190	120	205	130
5,000	130	90	145	100	170	110	180	110

Courtesy: Airtemp Div., Chrysler Corp.

119

Chapter 10

Chimneys and Fireplaces

CHIMNEYS

Chimneys are perhaps the least carefully built and most neglected parts of a house. Defective flues and chimneys are the second largest cause of fires in homes, according to the National Fire Protection Association. Clearly, chimneys merit careful inspection, particularly in older structures. An efficiently designed fireplace and chimney should provide a secure space for an open fire and a flue through which smoke and hot gases rise to the open air.

Today's chimney was developed about six hundred years ago. Long experience has demonstrated that a chimney's efficiency is determined by size and height in relation to the structure, plus tightness, smoothness, and shape.

A properly built chimney is ramrod-straight because any curve or angle interferes with the free rise of smoke, besides being a collection point for soot. Smoke and hot gases will eventually disintegrate ordinary mortar and cause leaks. Many older chimneys, built without a protective lining, function satisfactorily because the walls are extra thick. Nonetheless, a flue of brickwork and rough mortar or stones will lack the efficiency of a lined one.

Most building codes require a chimney's open shaft to be protected with fire clay lining which provides a tight, smooth surface for the uninterrupted flow of smoke. It also reduces the number of joints through which erosive smoke and gases can escape into the house. Inspecting the chimney at the smoke pipe opening will allow you to determine the thickness and see whether it has a flue lining.

If the chimney is only 4 inches thick—the thickness of a brick—and is unlined, it cannot be used safely. Without fire clay flue lining, two thicknesses of brick—8 inches from inside to outside—is the minimum for safe and satisfactory performance. Chimney walls of unreinforced concrete should be at least 8 inches thick. A small length of flue lining protruding from the top of an old chimney does not necessarily indicate the lining extends the full length. A short section of lining is frequently installed when an old chimney is repaired above the roof line.

Solid masonry is the safest and best material for chimney construction. In a frame house the chimney is best constructed on its own foundation. Because its concentrated weight tends to settle more than the house foundation and exterior walls, a chimney standing alone will not distort any part of the structure as would one to which framing members are fastened.

Allowing a chimney to rest on wooden beams or a wooden floor is an invitation to disaster. Incredibly, many houses in the United States have chimneys built in this manner. Nor should any wood be in direct contact with the chimney. Fire safety dictates a minimum space of 2 inches between the chimney and any woodwork.

A chimney functions most efficiently when located at or near the center of the house. With protection against frigid outside air, the flue draws a better draft and the heat is retained indoors. But this desirable arrangement is not always architecturally feasible.

Building codes usually require chimneys to extend high enough to avoid downdrafts caused by turbulent winds. A chimney should rise at least two feet above the ridge of a peak roof and three feet above a flat roof. Otherwise, the draft will be disrupted by eddies when the wind is deflected downward from the roof. Tree branches extending over the chimney will also interfere with the draft.

Raising the chimney to the correct height or covering it with an arched brick hood, the open ends parallel to the ridge, will markedly improve the draft. A flat stone hood may be used but is less attractive. Metal pipe extensions are widely used. Inexpensive and easy to install, they can be topped with a metal cowl that rotates with the wind to shield the flue from gusts.

Most pipe extensions are of galvanized tin which rusts in relatively short time. The more durable ones are made of aluminum or similar corrosion-resistant metals. Light in weight, these extensions must be the same size as the flue and be firmly fastened against strong winds. Terra-cotta chimney pots, common in Europe, will last indefinitely and are more decorative.

Gale force winds occasionally sway weaker chimneys, cracking open mortar joints at the roof line. Such rifts are particularly hazardous, for sparks from the flue may burn the woodwork. This problem does not exist where the upper part of a chimney, beginning well below its intersection with the roof, has walls at least 8 inches thick.

FLUES

A flue is a shaft in the chimney for the passage of smoke. If a soot fire occurs in the chimney, the safety of the house will depend on the soundness of the flue. Aside from preventing a good draft, a cracked flue is a fire hazard.

Each flue should have only one opening. If two heating units are connected to the same flue, a fire may ensue from sparks blown into one opening and out through the other. Both will also destroy each other's draft. When not in use, pipe openings should be closed with tightly-fitted metal caps and sealed with asbestos cement.

Sometimes a former owner of an older house has closed one or more flue openings and covered them with wallpaper. If the paper is not to be removed, these caps can nevertheless be detected by the slight bulges they form. Every room through which the chimney rises should be inspected for these improper caps, which may become red hot and set the house on fire.

A large proportion of fires traceable to chimneys are caused by careless stack connections. Fitting the pipe properly will substantially reduce the risk; even the smallest gap should be packed with asbestos cement to make an airtight connection. The pipe should be placed horizontally in the opening and remain flush with the flue lining. Extending the stack farther in the flue will interfere with the draft.

Because smoke pipe temperatures often rise well above 600° F., no stack should be closer than 18 inches to any woodwork unless it is protected against scorching. Fireproof asbestos pipe sleeves are commercially available. Even with such covering, the stack should not be nearer than 12 inches to wood or any other combustible material.

FIREPLACES

In many languages the word "hearth" is synonymous with home and family. This is not surprising because an open fire was and is the center of family enjoyment and camp life.

In northern climates a correctly built fireplace with a damper is a practical addition to other heating systems. In milder regions it can be the sole source of heat for a single room. The heating value of an ordinary fireplace is low, however, compared to the cheerful and cozy atmosphere it suffuses.

Equipped with a convection unit, a fireplace can heat a second room on the same level or an upper floor. This device contains hollow walls in which the heated air rises and flows out to the room. Placing the outlet in another room or the floor above will heat these areas.

A correctly built fireplace includes a properly designed damper to regulate the draft and reduce heat loss through the chimney in absence of a fire. Leaving the damper open in a modern house causes a needless waste of fuel. The damper consists of a cast iron frame and an adjustable hinged lid. It is installed between the fireplace and smoke chamber above and is always concealed by the brickwork. Some damper models are designed to support the brickwork or masonry over the opening.

INSPECTION

Chimneys sometimes are obstructed by birds' nests and fallen rubble, such as crumbled mortar and bricks. A visual inspection can be made in a smoke pipe opening with a bright-beamed flashlight and a mirror held at the correct angle. Any debris, if not packed too tightly, can be dislodged by moving a heavy chain up and down in the chimney.

Smoke-testing a chimney for leaks is best done by a mason skilled in chimney construction and repair. A fire is started with paper, excelsior, or soft wood. When it burns brightly, tar paper is added to produce a dense pillar of smoke. Then the flue at the top of the chimney is covered with a piece of water-soaked carpet. Forced to seek another outlet, the smoke will escape through the thinnest fissures, exposing their location. These leaks are then marked with chalk.

The size and number of leaks should determine the remedy. Smaller chinks may be filled with mortar. But cracked bricks and heavy leaks into adjacent flues or rooms indicate major repairs are necessary. A chimney in this condition is a grim fire threat. Particles of burning soot and sparks will easily pass through the cracks and alight on wood or some other combustible material. Correcting these defects is expensive.

If the house is to be heated by a gas-fired system, a masonry chimney is not essential. Virtually all building codes, including Underwriters' Laboratories, permit the connection of the system to a flue of sheet metal extending through the roof. The flue must be fully insulated with asbestos or comparable fireproof material.

Chapter 11

Home Protection

FIRE

Fire hazards lurk in nearly all homes. The potential causes are construction defects or the combustible contents of the home. Correcting flaws in construction is the builder's responsibility. Most cities and towns in America have codes to insure fire-safe construction, but these are not always strictly enforced. Combustible materials, such as wood, are banned from being placed too near heating units, smokestacks, chimneys, fireplaces, and hot air heating ducts. Faulty electrical wiring and chimneys without flues are also fire hazards.

Preventing fires that may be caused by combustible material in the house, however, devolves on the occupants. Many fires start in piles of trash, such as cartons, old papers, oily rags, and similar items. Rubbish should be removed frequently—the sooner, the better. It should not be allowed to pile up in the basement, beneath the stairs, in halls, in closets, or in the attic.

Flammable fluids are a major menace. Gasoline, naphtha, benzine, lacquers, and some paint and varnish removers ignite readily and burn violently. Some of these volatile liquids evaporate at room temperature; the invisible fumes waft along to the pilot light on the gas range and may result in a flash fire or explosion. A spark from the doorbell, telephone, or electric refrigerator may also cause gases to explode. Even a spark of static electricity generated merely by shifting clothing around in cleaning fluid may cause a flash fire. Kerosene or gasoline should never be used to start a fire. Oil-base paints stored in warm places may burn spontaneously. So will wax-saturated cloths or oily rags, which should be stored in metal containers.

Once a fire is underway inside a dwelling, it spreads by direct contact of flames with combustible objects, and by intensely hot gases and air that surge up stairways and through halls. In a house without fire stops, the searing gases will streak between floor joists and up wall

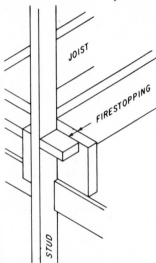

Fig. 11.1   Fire-Stop
Source—National
Forest Products Association

studs. One type of fire stop, a solid block of 2-inch wood cut to fit tightly between studs (Fig. 11.1) prevents heated gases from rising up the space between the walls.

Fire stops are important in the basement because a large percentage of fires start there. Covering the basement ceiling with fireproof gypsum board protects the exposed wood. Other measures include incombustible inorganic insulation blown between the walls and packed in framed openings around the chimney. If there are open spaces or flues between floors, wooden blocks should be placed between studs. Doors to the basement should fit snugly to reduce the amount of air feeding the fire.

Causes of Fire

Causes of fires in dwellings are shown in Table 5, prepared by the National Fire Protection Association:

TABLE 5

Smoking and matches	30%
Heating defects:	
Defective flues and chimneys	12%
Defective or overheated appliances	6%
Inadequate clearance from combustible materials	2%
Miscellaneous	1%
*Misuse of electricity:	
Fixed services	10%
Appliances or fixtures	2%
Exposure:	
Sparks on roof	6%
Other	2%
Inadequate rubbish disposal methods	4%
Kitchen hazards	4%
Hot ashes and coals	3%
Flammable liquids	2%
Lightning	2%
Spontaneous ignition	2%
Open fireplaces	2%
Children with matches	2%
Flammable decorations	1%
Candles and open flames (other than stove)	1%
Incendiary	1%
Vehicle fires	1%
Defective hot-water tanks	1%
Explosion (heat and power sources)	1%
Miscellaneous	2%
Total:	100%

* Insurance companies include an "escape clause" in fire protection policies, exempting them from payment if an inspection reveals the fire was caused by improper wiring.

Fire Alarm Systems

Home fire alarm systems are readily available at moderate prices. One model is a combined smoke and fire detector which emits a loud, howling alarm before smoke concentration becomes dangerous. The alarm is actuated when smoke interrupts a light beam shining on a photoelectric cell. A temperature rise above 135° F. will also trigger the alarm. The detector may be hung on any wall near the ceiling and plugged into the nearest electrical outlet. No batteries are required. A red bull's-eye light indicates the unit is in operation. The bulb will last about three years and can be easily replaced at nominal cost. To provide full protection, at least one alarm unit should be installed in every room, including the basement and the attic.

Another type of alarm is a closed circuit system that operates either on house current with a transformer or on two ordinary dry cell batteries. Because the unit draws only one-fifth of a milliampere (one-thousandth of an ampere), batteries will last up to eighteen months. The thermal detectors are wired in series to allow for any additional number throughout the house. Installed in the ceiling of every room, these detectors will sound an alarm when the temperature rises to 135°F. A special attic detector, designed for higher heat, is actuated when the temperature reaches 190°F. Since the alarm is on a separate battery, current is not used except when the bell rings. An extra weatherproof bell, inside or outside, will operate on the same alarm battery.

If a wire in the system's circuit is accidentally disconnected, broken, or the batteries are run down, the relay will drop out and sound the alarm. Batteries should be replaced once a year despite their probable longer life. A special power pack, consisting of a nickel cadmium battery, will last indefinitely since it draws only a trickle of electricity from the standard 110–120 volt outlet. The alarm can be sound-tested by pressing a button connected to the circuit.

A third model is a self-contained can filled with Freon, a harmless gas, under pressure. This device, which is hung on the wall, will sound a noisy alarm when the temperature rises to about 140°F. This model, like battery-operated units, will not be affected by a power blackout. If a fire is caused by defective wiring, the blown fuse or tripped circuit breaker will prevent an electrically-operated system from sounding an alarm.

Ionization Fire Detector

Maximum security fire protection is available to those who are not deterred by cost. Pyr-A-Larm is an ultra-sensitive system that sounds an alarm even *before* smoke is visible. The slightest rise in predetermined temperature also triggers the alarm. According to UL ratings, this device is about thirty-six times faster than a sprinkler system protecting the same area.

Operating on a patented ionization principle, Pyr-A-Larm reacts swiftly to the first trace of fire. Before an electric overload produces visible smoke, flame, or significant heat, it will generate very tiny combustion particles invisible to the human eye. Warmer than the surrounding air, these microscopic particles quickly rise to the ceiling where they disturb the delicate balance between two ionization chambers in the alarm. A highly sensitive cathode tube instantly signals a fire or zone indicator, actuating the alarm. When the alarm sounds, lights on the control panel pinpoint the zone of fire.

The smoke and heat detector in this alarm contains no moving parts and thus requires no adjustment or replacement after it sounds an alarm, because it automatically returns to normal operation. A small neon light at the detector's base visually indicates the system is in operation. All components are resistant to corrosion and vibration and should last indefinitely. Tests of the cathode tube indicate it will actuate about one hundred thousand alarms before wearing out. If a power failure occurs, this system will automatically switch to standby batteries.

Fire Extinguishers

Most fires, if detected early enough, can be put out with minimal damage. No home should be without at least one fire extinguisher for each floor. A garden hose permanently connected to a special faucet in the basement will be an effective extinguisher of wood, paper, or cloth fires. But water cannot be used on burning fat, oil, other flammable liquids, or electrical fires; only chemical extinguishers will snuff these out. Because water is one of the best conductors of electricity, an electrical fire must be fought with a non-conducting extinguisher. If used on such a fire, water may transmit the live current to the individual applying the water, causing possible shock or electrocution.

Use only fire extinguishers that list ratings by UL or Factory Mutual Laboratories (FM). Thus, the Class A extinguisher is limited to paper, wood, cloth, and similar materials; Class B is rated for all flammable liquids; and Class C is for electrical fires (Table 6).

For the home the B-C rated carbon dioxide and dry chemical extinguishers are recommended. The latter is specially treated sodium bicarbonate, and both can put out almost every type of household, car, or boat fire. Sprayed on a hot surface, these extinguishers form an oxygen-excluding blanket that will smother even deeply recessed fires. Both are clean and odorless in operation, and neither extinguisher will damage upholstery fabrics, drapes, or carpets.

TABLE 6

Fire Extinguisher Guide

Source—Walter Kidde & Company

Type of Agent →	Water	Foam	Carbon Dioxide	Regular Dry Chemical
Class A Fires PAPER, WOOD, CLOTH, etc., where quenching by water or insulating by Tri-Class general purpose dry chemical is effective.	YES Excellent. Water saturates material and prevents rekindling.	YES Excellent. Foam has both smothering and wetting action.	Small surface fires only.	Small surface fires only.
Class B Fires GASOLINE, OILS, PAINTS Burning liquids, cooking fats, etc., where smothering action is required.	NO Water will spread fire, not put it out.	YES Excellent. Smothering blanket does not dissipate, floats on top of spilled liquids.	YES Excellent. Carbon dioxide leaves no residue, does not affect equipment or food.	YES Excellent. Chemical powder smothers fire.
Class C Fires LIVE ELECTRICAL EQUIPMENT Fire in motors, switches, appliances, etc., where a nonconducting extinguishing agent is required.	NO Water, a conductor, should not be used on live electrical equipment.	NO Foam is a conductor and should not be used on live electrical equipment.	YES Excellent. Carbon dioxide is a non-conductor, leaves no residue, will not damage equipment.	YES Excellent. Chemical is a non-conductor; Screen of dry chemical shields operator from heat.

Carbon tetrachloride is also a B-C rated extinguisher, but it should not be used indoors because, upon contact with flame or a hot object, it changes to phosgene—a powerful lung irritant used in chemical warfare.

Fire Drills

Families who practice periodic fire drills have the highest survival rate. Before the drill, draw a floor plan that includes every room. With your family, visit each room and while there make an escape plan. Consider alternate routes. When planning escape or alternate routes from upstairs rooms, avoid use of interior stairs and open halls if possible. Rising heat and smoke often bank up in these areas.

Be sure children can open doors, windows, or screens to the escape routes. Assign responsibilities, such as assisting younger children or invalids, to adults and older children. A responsible person should be assigned the job of turning in the alarm to the Fire Department. All adults and school age children in your family should know the location and operation of the fire alarm box nearest your home. Because an alarm can also be sent by telephone, check your telephone book for specific instructions. Make sure that the one who discovers the fire will sound the alarm and alert the rest of the family or other occupants in the house. Have flashlights handy near the bedrooms to assist in escape. Check bedroom doors to see that they fit properly. Your life may depend on that door keeping out the fire.

Select a place outside the home for the family to meet after leaving the house. Try to choose an area well-lighted by a street light pole. It will then be easy to determine if all escaped. These suggestions were adapted from *Family Fire Drill,* a publication of the Fire Department of New York City.

Remaining in a burning house is very dangerous. Fire often races so swiftly that escape is cut off. If compelled to stay in a smoke-filled building, protect your nose and mouth with a wet cloth and crawl along the floor where the air is clearer. Never re-enter a burning house to save property. Only saving life justifies this personal risk. Leave the task of fire fighting to firemen.

In sparsely populated areas, the telephone is the fastest way to get help. If the occupants are awakened at night by an engulfing fire, no time may be left to use the phone. A car is the second best means to summon aid. If its ignition is locked, however, and the key is left in the burning house, the car will be useless. A duplicate ignition key in a magnetic metal container, secreted under a fender, will be useful in such an emergency. It may prevent total loss of your home.

Crippling injuries or death are often the tragic consequences of leaping from burning buildings. It will never be necessary to jump from an upper-story window if you take the simple precaution of installing a fire rope in every room. Manila rope one-inch in diameter, which has a minimum breaking strength of 9,000 pounds, should be securely tied to a stout metal eye screw twisted through the wall into a stud. To prevent the upright from splitting, bore a pilot hole slightly less than the shank's diameter and about one-half inch short of its length. Double-knot the rope every 15 inches to prevent skin burns from sliding down too fast. Be sure the line is long enough to reach the ground. Whether fastened to a stud in the closet or under the window, keep the rope coiled neatly so that it will not tangle when dropped from the window.

BURGLARY

Burglary of private homes ranks high on the list of crimes against property. Not, too many years ago, burglaries were largely confined to urban apartments and dwellings, but the use of cars today provides mobility to professional and novice criminals. Breaking and entering private homes may occur during the day when occupants are out, late at night, or in the early morning hours. A darkened house is always inviting to burglars.

A burglar's entrance is usually made by forcing a window to the basement or main floor, almost always by way of the rear yard. When operating after midnight, the suburban housebreaker cuts telephone wires as soon as he is inside—sometimes before he enters, if the wires are conveniently within reach. The after-midnight burglar, aware that people are in the house, invariably carries a weapon to assure his escape. As he moves about gathering loot, the intruder places chairs, stools, and similar objects in his wake so that any pursuer must trip over these obstacles and alert him.

Home Burglary Precautions

Professional criminals, unlike amateurs, seldom burglarize a house at random. Experience has taught them that paltry sums are not worth the risk. Before invading a home, they try to learn as much as possible about the family's habits, income, and the probable quantity of loot available. A frequently used subterfuge is the telephone survey, in which the "interviewer" can elicit a surprising amount of information from a trusting housewife. Clever thieves have learned enough to burglarize many a home during a family's absence with no risk of detection. Never give information to an unknown telephone voice purporting to interview you for some research project or market survey. Be equally circumspect with the phone canvasser who requests a personal appointment to show you merchandise. Ask for his or her phone number, then call back. More often than not, you may be given a false number. It is always best to buy at a reliable retail outlet or store.

No strange door-to-door salesman should be allowed in your house. He may be honest, but too many are thieves who want to "case" the premises, noting your material possessions. The night visitor should also be treated cautiously. If an unknown person appears at your door explaining that his car broke down, don't let him enter. Take his name and tell him that you will phone for assistance.

Before employing a maid, who will move about freely and be given charge of your children, be certain that you thoroughly check her references and background. The better employment agencies will do preliminary checking. Your obligation is greater when you hire a maid from a "situations wanted" ad. Female gang members often seek employment in upper income houses to assess potential loot for their confederates.

Keep a list of all your valuable objects and furnishings, and identifying numbers or markings that will aid the police to recover them in case of burglary. TV sets, appliances, cameras, watches, and similar items have serial numbers. Automobile thieves are skilled at repainting cars and changing serial numbers. Drop your business card or a similar identification down one or more door panels. Any dispute about a recovered stolen car will be quickly resolved if the door is taken apart and your identifying mark is found.

Always forbear discussing your expensive possessions with friends in public where strangers may overhear you and, above all, don't hoard unneeded valuables in your home. Securities, negotiable bonds, and large sums of money are safer in a bank.

Vacation Precautions

Unoccupied houses are enticing targets for intruders. Few blows are more distressing to a family returning from vacation than to find that their home has been ransacked by burglars or vandals. Houses that are unoccupied during a vacation are often bypassed by criminals when the family thoughtfully eliminates all indications of absence.

Stop all deliveries—milk, newspapers, mail, and parcel post—for the duration of your vacation. Notify your local police of your planned absence and where you can be contacted in an emergency. Also inform the police of crime deterrent devices you will install. At the same time request a trusted neighbor to keep an eye on your home and accept or pick up unexpected deliveries.

To burglars, a dark home means an easy mark. If you plan to be away, you can use automatic lighting devices to turn different lights on and off in various parts of the house. Automatic lighting can be controlled either by an electric timer or by a selenium cell, which is actuated by natural light. At dusk the cell turns on the lights, and at daybreak it turns them off.

Resist the temptation to have the local paper publish plans of your intended vacation. Burglars assiduously read social news. Except for the police and close friends, avoid discussing your trip with passing acquaintances or friendly strangers. Don't leave ladders, tools, or similar items lying about. These are excellent aids to breaking and entering.

Locks

Secure your outside doors with strong locks. Doors that simply lock upon closing are easily opened by a burglar using a strip of flexible metal or plastic. The best type is a deadlock which must be locked and unlocked with a key from the outside. Glass panel doors should be protected by double cylinder locks that must be key-operated on the inside as well as the outside.

Double cylinder locks are available in two models. The surface-mounted unit can be fastened with special screws that are slotted to turn only one way. Once firmly secured, such a lock cannot be unfastened with any screwdriver. The double cylinder mortise lock, as the name suggests, is recessed into the edge of the door without exposed screws.

Several types of cylinders are available for any deadlock. The single-bitted key is notched along one edge, and its lock is difficult to pick except by a skilled locksmith. Most criminals who prey on suburban dwellings lack the skill necessary to pick cylinder locks. They enter by breaking glass panels or window panes and reaching in to open the lock manually. But double cylinder locks which can be opened only by special keys are effective burglar deterrents.

A recently designed cylinder lock which combines pin tumblers with magnets has resisted lock-picking attempts by even the most skilled locksmiths. A coded set of magnets in its cylinder attract each other to create an immovable magnetic field. When the matching key is inserted into the lock it releases the magnets, allowing the mechanism to turn. Protected by a sealed plug, the magnets cannot be reached by any tool for picking. The alnico magnets are guaranteed for life and are not affected by slamming doors or dropped keys. This lock, patented as Miracle Lock, can replace all standard lock cylinders used in homes, and, since no special installation tools are necessary, the change can be made in five minutes by any locksmith or skilled handyman.

Windows and patio-type glass sliding doors are particularly vulnerable to the housebreaker and should be secured by key-controlled locks. Keys to the locks should be concealed but their location known and readily available to the occupants in case of fire.

Alarm Systems

Homes with watchdogs, especially large ones, are rarely burglarized. Intruders are quickly scared away by barking dogs. But during vacation trips, when the dog is away with the family or in a kennel, there is no substitute for an intrusion detection device. Burglar alarms range from a battery-operated bell set to ring when a door or window is opened to sophisticated electronic and ultrasonic systems.

A typical electronic alarm consists of a master unit attached to the front door it protects. It also serves as the master control center for accessory devices to protect any number of doors and windows throughout the house. Operated by low voltage current or a self-contained battery, the master unit has a built-in alarm and protects the dwelling whether occupants are home or away. A fourteen-second delay feature permits family members to enter without tripping the warning clamor. The system is easily controlled by a cylinder-type removable on/off key.

All remote control units—simple magnetic devices—protecting every door and window are activated merely by a single plug to the master control center. If any of the connecting wires are cut or broken, the master alarm will automatically sound. A window or door forced open will also activate the alarm and closing them will not stop the warning sound. Only a special key can turn off the alarm; otherwise the piercing blare will continue for at least twenty minutes, panicking the burglar and alerting neighbors and police.

Another useful attachment is a "panic button" for bedside protection. Pressing this button will activate the alarm to shatter the night silence. Since burglars are constrained to operate stealthily, any warning din terrifies them, for it usually leads to detection and arrest.

Electronically wired rubber or neoprene doormats, identical in appearance to standard types, may be set at all door entrances. As soon as anyone reaches the door, an alarm will sound.

The "Telemergency," a silent dialing unit, can be wired to the telephone junction box, while the device itself is concealed in a closet or desk drawer. When tripped by any type of alarm system, panic button, or step-on-mat, Telemergency promptly dials the first number recorded on the tape, usually that of the police. When the phone is answered, it may report: "There is a burglary taking place at 500 Elm Street. Rush police help immediately. This is an automatic dialing system triggered by an intruder." This recorded message will be repeated twice.

Telemergency will dial up to four telephone numbers. If the phoned number is busy, the next prerecorded number is automatically dialed. A radio or wireless remote control can also be used to trigger the alarm. Telemergency procedures can be applied to fire alarm systems and other emergency services, such as hold-ups in the home, boiler failure, and refrigerator failure.

Ultrasonic alarm systems operate on the principle that movement disturbs sound wave patterns. The protected area is filled with ultrasonic sound waves barely above the range of human hearing. A highly stable oscillator generates microwaves that radiate by remote detector to saturate a given area. Any human movement in this area will change the sound wave pattern, setting off an alarm. (The alarm is not set off by small animals.) No intruder can escape detection. A burglar cannot break a glass pane, or open even unlocked windows or doors without triggering an alarm. Most units are tamperproof; any attempt to silence them triggers an alarm siren or gong. Some models have an automatic telephone dialer which silently makes up to five emergency calls that can relay five separate prerecorded messages to different police numbers if one is busy. A message may also be prerecorded to alert a neighbor by phone.

Ultrasonic home model alarms are similar in size and shape to table radios, and their installation is simple. One line from the unit is plugged into an electrical outlet, the other into a nearby telephone jack. The ultrasonic unit itself is placed on a table, desktop, or book-case in the room or area to be protected. Models are available to protect medium or large rooms. Turning a key will immediatly activate the unit, filling the area, including doors and windows, with ultrasonic energy.

Chapter 12

Home Improvements

Homes more than twenty-five years old usually are in need of some major repairs. Heating equipment this old will soon need replacement, especially if it is a coal furnace that has been converted to gas or oil. Hot water tanks seldom last beyond ten or fifteen years. Galvanized pipes become choked with rust, eroding through within twenty years. Asphalt shingle roofing, unless heavyweight, has an average life of twenty to twenty-five years in the cooler northern areas. In the South, these shingles require replacement after fifteen to twenty years. Wooden exteriors must be painted every five to ten years.

The advantages of an older home are not invalidated by these unavoidable repairs. Often a dwelling can be bought at a price that will compensate for costly improvements. Even a new home entails expenses in maintenance and alterations.

PITFALLS OF HOME IMPROVEMENT

Before undertaking expensive repairs, the home owner should be aware that the home improvement industry is rife with swindlers and incompetent bunglers, because most states or localities are without laws to license such contractors and servicemen. It is not surprising therefore that persons capable of fraud and deceit are attracted to the home improvement business, which grosses more than 11 billion dollars a year. In 1965 the state of Maryland enacted a law to license home repair firms that has since proved to be effective.

In an industry where inflated prices and shoddy workmanship are disproportionately high, the careful home owner will take the necessary precautions against racketeering and incompetence. Responsible house-inspection experts will examine your home for whatever repairs may be needed and provide a written report. Their fees are seldom above sixty-five dollars but you will be well repaid by their professional advice. These experts are listed in the yellow pages of the telephone directory under Building Inspection Service.

Home improvement swindlers employ the modus operandi common to all con men. Their typical victim is a home owner who hopes to obtain something for nothing or at a tiny fraction of its actual worth; other candidates are simply endowed with unlimited gullibility. By tailoring their approach to fit the season, usually the first signs of spring, a motley collection of itinerant hucksters and repairmen will appear and offer assorted products, such as carports, patios, shade trees, or siding. The Better Business Bureau records indicate that home repair frauds are the number one gyp in the spring. An estimated $500 million is obtained annually by these roving con men.

Other practitioners in springtime larceny appear in trucks to offer rich topsoil guaranteed to revitalize lawns weakened by the rigors of winter. A basket of black "humus" is strewn on the lawn to prove how little is required. Each basket is quoted at a dollar or two, but an unwary home owner, who does not have a sharp eye, may be charged one hundred dollars or more. This "humus" is usually waste material from a chemical plant, often consisting of substances poisonous to plant life.

Another flourishing racketeer is the door-to-door "termite inspector" who "discovers" these insects in all parts of the house. (He has merely flung them about during the inspection when the owner was not watching.) More adept at defrauding than at pest extermination, he will pour a worthless solution in the soil around the dwelling before extracting a handsome fee.

In the wake of the termite "expert" may appear the wandering "tree surgeon," spouting a pseudo-scientific jargon to befuddle the owner into believing his trees are dying. A tree that required many years to grow can be mutilated by one of these men in an hour. Countless shade trees in America have been destroyed in this manner.

Siding the exterior walls of a house with aluminum is particularly appealing to owners of older homes. Posing as a representative of a reputable manufacturer, this type of trickster will notify the owner that his home has been selected as a model to be re-sided with aluminum, because its location is intended to stimulate consumer interest. The home owner is promised that, besides the free siding, the company will pay him a substantial cash commission. If the prospective victim hesitates, he may be paid a cash advance as an inducement. Once he accepts, he is asked to sign several papers placed before him, in one of which he offers his house as security against the cost of the siding.

After it is too late, the home owner learns that the salesman did not represent any of the large aluminum companies. He also discovers that instead of obtaining free siding, he must pay twice the price charged by reputable contractors. Commissions to the salesmen for each contract may range up to $1,500.

One effective way to combat such frauds is with an FHA-insured loan. Under FHA regulations, a contractor will not be paid until the home owner signs a completion certificate which states he is satisfied with the work. Never sign such a certificate until you are satisfied the work has been done in accordance with the contract. The contractor cannot be paid without your signature. Also be careful not to sign a completion certificate that may be deftly slipped in with the sales order.

The FHA has compiled a nationwide list of firms who have been guilty of dishonest and shoddy performance, banning them from doing work in the future with a loan by this government agency. Many fraudulent contractors operate under changing business names and often move to other localities. But the FHA keeps track of them with a blacklist containing thousands of names. Any home owner may check his contractor's record against the FHA list.

THE CONTRACTOR

Although most home improvement contractors are conscientious, this multi-billion dollar industry is murky with operators who shift easily from one corporate name to another, leaving botched homes and unfinished work for which they have already been paid. Almost none can be sued because they operate as a corporation, which can be quickly formed when at least three persons file a certificate of incorporation with the Secretary of State or other designated public official and pay a filing fee of about sixty-five dollars. A corporation is recognized as a separate entity or body by law, and none of its officers is responsible for debts after the firm is dissolved in bankruptcy.

It is not unusual for miscreant contractors to have several corporations operating in relays, dissolving one when it becomes a target for lawsuits by irate home owners and resuming business under another corporate name. That some 98 percent of the contractors doing residential work exclusively are ineligible for bonding to guarantee satisfactory performance attests to the marginal character of the home improvement industry. Performance Bonds and Labor and Material Bonds are largely given to builder-contractors undertaking construction of public projects, commercial and industrial buildings, and tract developers. For a premium, the bonding company guarantees completion of the contract if the contractor for any reason is unable to finish the work.

Before hiring a contractor, especially for a major improvement, check his reputation with the Better Business Bureau and the local Chamber of Commerce. Not every instance of fraud is reported to these organizations, but if a contractor has left a sizeable number of wrathful home owners in his wake, it is likely that someone has filed a complaint. If the work is to be done with an FHA loan, your lender will submit the contractor's name to be checked against the FHA's list of individuals banned for dishonesty or incompetence, or both. The lending agency itself is reasonably well-informed about local contractors.

A contractor worthy of the title should have a permanent business address. Since he presumably buys from local building materials dealers, you should check his credit standing with them. If they refuse him credit and demand cash payments, bypass him. Reputable contractors have charge accounts with their suppliers.

Ask the contractor to give you the names of three or more home owners for whom he worked. Visit the addresses to inspect his work. Satisfied customers will be pleased to recommend a contractor who gave them full value for their money. Sometimes a contractor who never left a customer satisfied may give you a friend or confederate's name and address. Such a contractor will try to talk you into a "fantastic" bargain. But the best bargain is a first-class job, which you should be able to determine.

Home Improvement Estimate

Aware that you are to make a decision involving hundreds or thousands of dollars, a reliable firm should assist you in judging their efficiency. They will not offer to arrange for a larger loan than needed for the job, promising to slip you the amount over the written agreement price. Since a wide range of products are made for the home improvement industry, they should be offered for your selection. Differences in quality will be explained to assist you in making a decision to fit your ability to pay.

A legitimate contractor is interested in giving you your money's worth. He will not try to hook you with such bait as "I am a special factory representative in your community, as part of our advertising campaign . . . " or "I will use your home for a model . . ." then promise to pay a commission on every sale resulting from your "model home." The "few simple agreement papers" you sign may jeopardize your ownership.

Always seek several competitive bids which will give you the opportunity to check and compare. Estimates by reputable contractors should not vary too much from each other. The lowest bid will not necessarily assure good workmanship or materials. A contractor whose estimate is substantially lower than other estimates, may have made an "error." Perhaps he lacks skill, or he may intend to cheat you for "finer materials" that are not included in the agreement, or he will simply use shoddy materials. But sometimes the very low bidder is a new, reputable contractor who wants his first job and bids low to win it.

Since house construction is not an exact science, the contractor's substandard work and materials may remain undetected for years. When defects become painfully evident, the "corporation" might no longer exist, and the contractor may be operating behind the name of another "paper" company.

Satisfy yourself that the contractor is fully insured to protect you against claims by injured workers, visitors, or passersby. Ask for his Certificate of Insurance which should list workmen's compensation and public liability insurance (personal and property). Where local laws require a contractor to obtain a license, verify his number with the bureau authorized to enforce the ordinance.

Home Improvement Contract

Any contract for costly alterations or remodeling should contain: (1) A detailed description of the project. (2) Materials and labor specifications. (3) Estimated costs. (4) Time required for completion. (5) Type of warranties, if any, given by suppliers of the products and materials he will install, and who will service the warranties—the contractor or the supplier. (6) Plans or sketches of the proposed work. (7) Description of all necessary building or other permits to be secured by the contractor, the fees to be paid and by whom. (8) Guarantee of quality of workmanship. (9) Total price of the work. (10) Method of payment.

Be sure the contract provides for removal of all rubbish, leaving your premises in broom-clean condition. Without a detailed description of the work in writing, misunderstandings can easily arise. A duplicate of this agreement should be given to you *at the time you sign.*

Initial discussions with the contractor usually revolve around details of the work to be done. Note his suggestions and discuss them thoroughly; take your time in reaching a decision. As the work progresses changes may be suggested and substitutions requested. These should be in writing. Noting all changes in writing will preclude future disagreements because the contract protects both home owner and contractor.

Most home owners who have dealt with contractors can attest that they frequently disregard starting and finishing dates. Schedules may be interrupted for a number of legitimate reasons—weather, strikes, etc. Too often, however, the contractor will undertake other smaller jobs, aware that you are under contract and cannot hire another firm. Have a clause added to the contract for penalty payments to be paid by the contractor for each day the work remains unfinished beyond the agreed completion date, allowing for unavoidable interruptions.

Most major home improvement work is paid for in periodic installments. Some home owners prefer to take a loan from the bank to pay cash to the contractor. Usually the agreement with the contractor provides for periodic payments—one-third down at the signing of the contract; one-third when the work is half finished; and one-third upon completion. Some contractors habitually ask home owners for payments before they are due. Your interests will be best protected by making payments as agreed upon in the contract. Adhering to this schedule will discourage the contractor from wandering off to side jobs while neglecting yours.

Many pleasant relationships between contractor and home owner end acrimoniously when the latter is billed at a much higher price than that originally agreed upon. Some contractors will deliberately lower their estimate because they intend to bilk a home owner for so-called better materials and extras. Misunderstandings with honest contractors arise when the home owner requests changes and different materials after the work starts. You can avoid dispute by specifying that all materials and workmanship should be at the contract price, and that no extra costs will be added unless authorized in writing with an agreed price for every item plus labor costs.

In case you are doubtful about a contractor, ask him to enter the contract individually as a guarantor for his corporation, which will make him personally liable even if his company dissolves. This practice is quite usual in commercial contracts that involve large sums of money. If the contractor refuses your request, look for one whom you can trust.

No responsible home improvement contractor can give a lifetime or an unconditional guarantee, since few items are made that can be assured to last so long. The term "fully guaranteed" offers no actual protection and is frequently used as bait. A reliable firm will list in writing precisely what is guaranteed and for what length of time. A guarantee against defective materials and workmanship is especially important.

Chapter 13

Special Types of Houses

THE MOBILE HOME

The mobile home industry has expanded enormously in recent years. In the early 1940s two out of three trailers were put together in rear yard shops; now several hundred manufacturers prefabricate complete trailer homes. Government census takers list mobile homes like any other house.

More than 5 million Americans live in mobile homes in 25,000 special parks or use trailers for their original function—traveling. Some of the people who use trailers are military personnel and construction workers who are mobile because of their work. Others are vacationers who prefer this mode of travel for economic reasons. But the two largest groups of trailer dwellers are young married people in need of comparatively inexpensive housing and retired couples.

About 150,000 mobile homes are produced yearly, exceeding the number of standard prefabricated houses. Coaches range in price from about $6,000 to $15,000, and custom-made units may cost as much as $50,000. Prices include all living facilities—kitchen range, refrigerator, dinette and bedroom furniture, and sanitary accommodations. Linens and tableware are extra. For those who prefer to travel in their own homes without a trailer hitch, self-propelled units are available.

Luxury coaches are equipped with built-in television, central air-conditioning, dishwashers, an intercom system, and automatic clothes dryers. Some are as much as 60 feet long and 12 feet wide and must be transported to their sites by heavy-duty trucks or railroad flat cars. Their rubber-tired wheels are removed when the home is permanently set in place.

Expandable mobile homes are available for families who may need extra space. Manufactured in sections that telescope during transit and open out when on site, these flexible units afford an extra room or add as much as eight feet in width to a living room or bedroom. When opened in full, the expandable home is L-shaped. Those with greater space may form an F-shaped unit.

Some 75 percent of all single homes under $12,500 are mobile units. Most remain stationary for long periods in trailer parks where water, gas, electricity, and other facilities are available at monthly rentals of $40 and up. Throughout the United States there are many trailer parks where mobile homes are permanently set up on concrete pads with gardens, terraces, and other accommodations. These permanent trailer homes have become so popular that many communities now have strict zoning regulations regarding their location.

Although banks and other lenders formerly denied loans for mobile homes, they now grant mortgages but not on terms similar to those for conventional dwellings, because a mobile home is considered chattel or movable property, not real property. A down payment of 25 percent on such a mortgage is not unusual. But a mobile unit's price does not include land, the foundation, and other expenses necessary for the purchase of a conventional house. Like a car, it can be bought within an hour.

A well-maintained house appreciates in value over the years, but a mobile home does not; its value predictably depreciates. Mortgage loans are usually for periods of five to seven years, rarely more than ten years. Unlike a conventional dwelling, a mobile home can be driven away or stolen. These are some of the factors which cause interest rates to be discounted in advance, often amounting to 15 percent or higher. As mobile homes age, they are sold like secondhand cars.

Criteria for Choosing a Mobile Home

Choose a mobile home the way you would choose any dwelling. There is no substitute for comparison shopping. Makers of mobile homes offer descriptive booklets of their products. You can get the names and addresses of these manufacturers from the Mobile Home Manufacturers Association, 20 North Wacker Drive, Chicago, Illinois, 60606.

A mobile home, new or used, constructed of shoddy materials or poor workmanship is never a bargain, however low the price. California seems to be the only state with a code to provide minimum standards of protection. Most better quality mobile homes bear the Gold Seal Emblem of the Mobilehome Craftsman's Guild, which indicates that they meet prescribed standards for materials and construction. The majority of reputable dealers belong to the Mobilehome Dealers National Association.

Visit mobile home parks where you will have a good opportunity to inspect and compare different models. Do not hesitate to discuss your intention to buy such a home with residents. You can learn a great deal from these friendly conversations.

THE WATERFRONT HOME

Many fishermen and boatmen plan to own their dwelling on the waterfront, with an adjoining dock. To these enthusiasts the advantages are obvious, but such ownership entails troublesome drawbacks. A primary requisite to owning a boat moored at your own dock is the financial means to maintain the pleasures of such a life.

Repair and maintenance costs of waterfront property are far higher than those for an inland home. Among the numerous expenses are such indispensable items as catwalks and bulkheads, which are recurrent annual expenses. The cost of replacement of lost topsoil and fill due to erosion, and other lawn and shrub damages caused by high water must also be considered. Salt water dampness, mildew, and rust necessitate periodic replacement of machinery and tools.

In northern latitudes, the pleasant life in a waterfront house usually ends with the autumnal storms. Surging seas and bone-chilling winter winds cause extreme dampness. Looking forward to next summer's idyllic existence may compensate for winter harshness, but the prospective waterfront home buyer should ponder the costs.

Waterfront home ownership involves an uninsurable risk, that of damage resulting from crashing high tides and flood waters. Especially distressing is the frequent ruinous loss caused when a hurricane rips away the roof, allowing the cascading rains to flood the interior. A sound insurance policy will cover such wind loss, but not if a high tide or flood causes the same damage. If you plan to buy waterfront property, be aware of the losses you may have to sustain.

VACATION HOMES

More than 2 million Americans now own a second home. These range from mansions to modest cottages. Every year the number is increased by some 150,000 new owners, according to a survey by the Jim Walter Corporation, a leading builder of vacation homes.

This survey also indicates that the factors contributing to the increased demand for second homes are: The rapid increase in population and increased urbanization (70 percent of the population resides in 5,000 urban centers); improved highway systems making remote areas more readily accessible; increased income; shorter work week with longer vacations and more three-day weekends; early retirement and longer life span.

The desirability of the more relaxed atmosphere of rural or semi-rural settings, but a reluctance to forgo completely the income opportunities and conveniences of urban life, has given impetus to the construction of leisure homes. The average second-home owner maintains a residence in or near the city for the work week and a second home, slightly less than three hours away, for use on weekends and during vacations.

Where to Build or Buy

Every state in the United States contains some desirable areas in which to build a leisure home. The most popular vacation areas seem to coincide with the most populous areas of the country, with New England having the most vacation homes, followed by the Great Lakes states.

Selecting a desirable location depends on your preferences. An oceanfront beach house would not appeal to a hunter any more than a western ranch setting would to a boating enthusiast. Unless you have already decided on the area for your vacation home, begin by studying road maps to see what appeals to you. Visit the location you like best. Check the roads, proximity, and direct access from your first home; explore areas off the main road. When you know the area well, speak to the local real estate brokers and look at their offerings. Buy the local papers and look at the real estate offerings in the classified ads. If prices are given, you will be able to estimate property values in the area.

No site should be selected without considering the availability of electricity, water, and sewerage. If you choose a remote section, away from recreation communities, you will probably have to drill a well for drinking water and install a cesspool or septic tank. You may even have to produce your own electricity with a gasoline generator. In almost all parts of the United States, however, electric service is available from private or government utilities, or Rural Electric Association co-ops.

If telephone service is available you may want to have one installed, but, if not, you should know the location of a phone for emergency calls. At least one general store selling essential items should be nearby. Access to the property should also be considered, not only for your convenience, but because construction materials and workmen must be transported to the site.

If you build your home, unless you select a relatively flat parcel of land, at least part of the site will have to be cleared for the house. Since this may entail the hiring of earth-moving equipment, plan in advance to leave as many trees as possible for future shade and beauty. Deck areas can be built around trees to retain some of the natural setting.

Type of Home

The demand for low-cost, simple, easy-to-care-for vacation homes, which can be built quickly, has been met by the construction industry with new and imaginative concepts in design and materials. Construction costs for the vacation home are generally lower than

Fig. 13.1   Vacation Home   Source—Master Plan Service, Inc.

for a conventional home because the vacation house has no basement and most interior finishes are eliminated. Construction materials are the double-duty type for both interior and exterior use. The double purpose sheathing/siding usually has good insulating qualities, and at a later date can easily be covered with finish materials.

Since interior finishes are usually omitted, the exposed framing, studs, and other structural members become part of the interior design (Fig. 13.1). Spaces between studs can be equipped with shelves to provide storage space; simple furnishings and extensive use of bright colored paints are the general rule.

Balconies and decks which increase living space are also attractive architectural features. Skylights and clerestory windows provide light. Sliding or hinged panels of wood or laminated or textured materials offer space flexibility.

Emphasis upon structural simplicity has led to widespread acceptance of the "roof" house for leisure homes. Popular in ski and mountain areas is the simple A-line house, because its design is excellent for shedding snow. The mansard roof house provides more space within its attic-type interior. It is also popular in northern climates. Beach houses often utilize camp-type construction with sliding screens and canvas blinds.

Most leisure homes are constructed on concrete slabs but, if built on piling off the ground or over water, the space underneath can be used to park cars or boats, or as a shaded recreation area (Fig. 13.2).

The majority of vacation homes today have plumbing and electrical conveniences. Required heating is provided by portable heaters or prefabricated, freestanding fireplaces.

The Jim Walter Corporation, which builds leisure houses, reports that most people want a second home suitable for year-round use, with sufficient sleeping area for guests and a large central place where family and guests can conveniently gather. Today's vacation homes are 80 to 90 percent completed on the inside when sold whereas twenty years ago most vacation homes were simple shells.

Vacation home communities are widely promoted in resort areas and are developed in the same manner as suburban housing tracts. They offer planned recreational activities, clubhouses, tennis courts, swimming pools, teen clubs, and similar facilities. Fees or dues are charged for use of most facilities and club membership.

In selecting a leisure home, the same standards should be used

Fig. 13.2   Vacation Home on Piling   *Source—Jim Walter Corporation*

as in evaluating a conventional house; there are no substitutes for good materials and sound construction.

The Vacation-Retirement Home

The vacation home intended for future use as a retirement home should have a frame as well constructed as that of a conventional house and be large enough to provide comfortable living facilities when converted. The minimal camp-type beach house would not be suitable for long-term use as a retirement home without extensive revisions.

All interior finishes of a vacation-retirement home except those considered absolutely essential may be eliminated at the time of construction to lower the costs. Although the home may be completed in stages over a long period of time, be sure that the local zoning ordinances permit occupancy of a partially finished house.

If the activity of a planned recreation community does not fit in with your living pattern, be sure you do not build or buy your house in an area so isolated that you will have difficulty securing required supplies or services in off-seasons. Land prices are generally higher in easily accessible areas but these costs are offset by the conveniences that are available.

Financing

Most recreational community developers require low down-payments and provide assistance in securing mortgages that extend for terms of five to twenty years. Banks and other conventional lenders are often reluctant to arrange financing for second homes. There are some builders of quality vacation homes who offer good design and construction, and up to 100 percent financing. No down payment is required of qualified property owners, and mortgage terms are up to twelve years.

Part II

Financing Your Home

Chapter 14

Initial Considerations
in Home Financing

HOW MUCH SHOULD YOU PAY
FOR A HOME?

Banks and other lenders do not adhere to any rigid formula in granting a loan, nor does the FHA when it insures credit. There are sound reasons why lenders largely ignore the old rule that one can safely buy a house equal to two and one-half times his annual gross income.

Before approving a loan, lending agencies consider several factors: the borrower's ability to repay the money in uninterrupted installments; his standard of living in relation to his income; and his credit standing, that is, his past record in paying bills.

If a borrower chooses a house for which he will be unable to pay the loan regularly after all other living expenses plus taxes are paid, his application will be denied. That he has an excellent reputation for paying bills is irrelevant. He will be advised to buy a home at a lower price for which he can meet all recurrent costs without undue deprivation.

As the FHA explains: "No ready formula can be used to relate either housing expense or purchase price to a prospective home owner's income. FHA considers both the borrower's income and his age, but only as they relate to other factors that affect his ability to repay the loan."

One of the least desirable credit risks is the chronically delinquent payer. Credit companies have extensive files listing recalcitrant payers. Within this category are those whose expenses habitually exceed their income. Evidence is overwhelming that such persons do not mend their ways when buying a house.

An applicant may earn enough to easily pay the loan after all basic living needs are met. But if he and his family live extravagantly, hosting expensive parties, buying high-priced cars, spending without stint for clothes and pleasure jaunts, and thus leaving nothing to save, lenders will tend to doubt his ability to pay a long-term loan.

Most of these conditions will be mitigated in varying degree by the amount of the down payment. If a buyer pays cash in the amount of $24,000 or 80 percent for a $30,000 house, he will usually receive a 20 percent loan or $6,000. In this case the lender's investment is very secure. To be considered for any mortgage loan, dubious credit risks must place a much larger down payment than others.

Each buyer can easily decide how much he can afford: if your estimated annual costs for the new dwelling are the same or slightly higher than your current housing expenses, you will encounter no difficulty. Should the estimated annual expenses markedly exceed your present dwelling costs, you should seek a lower-priced house. See the Financial Checklist, Appendix II, for guidance.

WHY YOU NEED A LAWYER

Almost every mistake in a real estate transaction is expensive. Recognizing the ancient maxim, "Let the buyer beware," the law presumes that the purchaser has fully examined the property and knowingly accepted its defects, if any. If certain conditions are promised orally by the seller but omitted from the contract, the buyer is without legal redress.

Unless you clearly understand the nature of binders, contracts, and other legal documents essential to the purchase of real property, you should retain a lawyer; not any attorney, but one who has had extensive experience in negotiating real estate contracts.

Lawyers do not advertise; however, if you live in or near a large city, contact the local Legal Referral Service (sometimes called the Lawyer or Attorney Reference Service) that functions in two-hundred urban areas with full support of the bar associations. One or more names will be given to you if you request a lawyer with real estate experience. In areas without a Legal Referral Service, the best source of information is the Bar Association, which usually is located in the county court building. In smaller communities, the local lawyer will usually be a general practitioner, but he most likely will have some experience in real property contracts.

An occasional seller may suggest that you forgo the expense of having a lawyer because his attorney will efficiently guide the transaction to an amicable closing. The seller may be well-intentioned, but you may later learn that you made a mistake. It always costs much less for a lawyer to prevent you from blundering into trouble than to extricate you from your difficulties.

For those who buy a house in a different section or state, a competent real estate lawyer is indispensable. Referring to the quandary in which so many home buyers find themselves, Richard Haydock, executive director of the Legal Referral Service in Manhattan, New York City, commented: "If I were buying a home in a strange area where I knew nobody, I would visit a bank that is *not* financing my mortgage. I'd find out the name of its lawyer and retain him, confident that my interests would be well-protected."

Chapter 15

Mortgages

Pledging real estate to guarantee repayment of a loan dates back to early times. If a debtor stopped payment, his creditor became owner of the pledged property. Modern mortgage law, derived from old English practices, operates in a similar manner. A person who borrows funds for the purchase of a house gives the lender a note or bond unconditionally promising to repay the loan with interest. In addition, the borrower gives his creditor a mortgage (a legal document) pledging the property as security for the loan.

The mortgage (literally *dead deed*) remains dormant so long as the debtor repays his loan. If he defaults, the deed "comes to life" and authorizes the creditor to acquire the debtor's property as his own. Property may be sold during the term of a mortgage, but it is the buyer's responsibility to examine public records for evidence of a mortgage lien. Borrowers do not "pay on a mortgage" but on the bond or note they sign.

Before the great depression in 1929, mortgage loans were granted for relatively short terms, seldom longer than five years. Down payments were high, often up to 50 percent of the purchase price. Only the interest was paid; none of the money was allocated to reduce the principal, which became payable in one lump sum on the due date. Only savings and loan associations practiced the sound policy of *amortized* (self-liquidating) home loans that are standard today.

Home owners who were unable to repay the loan when due were given short term renewals, provided they did not fall behind in payment of interest. Lack of money to liquidate the principal led harried borrowers to second, even third mortgages with escalating rates of interest. When sorely in need of funds, the banks demanded full payment on loans as they became due, but the unemployed home owners were unable to continue payments even on the interest. The homes that were foreclosed by the banks remained unsold. Glutted with unsalable houses and unable to pay their depositors, many banks failed.

THE AMORTIZED MORTGAGE

To help extricate the nation from its crisis, Congress established the Federal Housing Administration in 1934. Under the FHA an amortized mortgage was developed and is still widely used today. In contrast to the unsound previous loans, an amortized mortgage provides for fixed monthly payments over a long period of time. The total amounts of the loan and interest payable are added together, then divided into equal monthly payments.

Each payment reduces the principal, and a portion is applied to the total interest due. The greater part of the monthly payments in the first few years is applied to interest. In later years the larger share of the payments reduce (amortize) the principal. The amortized mortgage is used by the majority of lending institutions in the United States today.

The principal sources of mortgage loans are the banks, the mortgage brokers, and the life insurance companies which provide the conventional, or privately financed loans, and the governmental agencies, such as the Federal Housing Administration (FHA) and the Veterans Administration (VA).

FEDERAL HOUSING ADMINISTRATION (FHA) LOANS

Since its inception the FHA has underwritten mortgage and loan insurance amounting to 107 billion dollars for 8 million homes, and through this agency more than 37 million families have been able to improve their housing conditions.

The FHA does not lend money but insures mortgage loans made by banks, building and loan associations, insurance companies, and other approved lenders. These insured loans enable buyers to finance their homes on more generous terms than would otherwise be available. Only the lender—not the home owner—is protected against loss on the loan. The FHA does not provide house plans or build structures.

The FHA uses a percentage scale to determine the amount of the mortgage loan. Insured loans on one-family houses, approved by FHA for construction, require low down payments, as indicated in Table 7:

TABLE 7

FHA SCALE

FHA APPRAISED VALUE	DOWN PAYMENT	AMOUNT AND % OF LOAN	
up to $15,000	3%	97%	
15,000	$ 450	$14,550	97%
20,000	1,000	19,000	95%
23,000	1,600	21,400	93%
25,000	2,000	23,000	92%
28,000	2,600	25,400	90.7%
30,000	3,000	27,000	90%
35,000	5,000	30,000	85.7%

Down payment requirements for houses built without FHA approval before or at the beginning of construction, but which have been completed less than one year before application for approval, would be somewhat higher. Down payments for a house of this type are shown in Table 8.

The down payment represents the difference between the amount of the insured mortgage and the purchase price of the home. Sometimes the FHA appraised value of a house and its purchase price may not agree. The FHA will insure a mortgage only at the percentage scale of the home's appraised value, *not* a percentage of the purchase price, unless the purchase price is *less* than the appraised value. If a borrower pays $30,000 for a house which is FHA approved before construction and appraised at $25,000, the maximum mortgage loan will be 92 percent of $25,000 or $23,000. He will therefore be required to make a down payment of the difference or $7,000.

TABLE 8

FHA APPRAISED VALUE	DOWN PAYMENT	AMOUNT AND % OF LOAN	
up to $20,000	10%	90%	
23,000	$2,600	$20,400	88.7%
25,000	3,000	22,000	88%
28,000	3,600	24,400	87.1%
30,000	4,000	26,000	86.7%
35,000	5,000	30,000	85.7%

FHA repayment terms extend to thirty years. If the house was constructed under FHA or VA inspection, the term may be as long as forty years, permitting low monthly mortgage payments for families with limited budgets. These regular payments include repayment of part of the loan, interest, amounts for mortgage insurance premiums, fire and other property insurance, taxes and other special assessments.

Interest rates vary, depending upon supply and demand of mortgage money. In 1970, the maximum interest rate for FHA loans was set at $8\frac{1}{2}$ percent, including an insurance premium of $\frac{1}{2}$ of 1 percent to protect the lender's investment, thus raising the rate to 9 percent.

Prepayment privileges are included with every FHA mortgage. In any calendar year the home owner may prepay up to 15 percent of his original mortgage loan. If, for example, it amounts to $15,000, he is allowed to prepay up to $2,250 of the principal each year. Borrowers of conventional mortgages, on the other hand, are usually penalized with additional costs if they want to prepay their loans.

Before the FHA approves a mortgage for a new home, the builder must guarantee that the structure conforms substantially to the plans and specifications upon which the agency based its appraisal. This safeguard for the home owner extends one year either from the time title is taken or the house first occupied. The builder is constrained to make the necessary repairs at his own expense. Those who refuse are banned from selling homes with FHA mortgages. The damages must result from defective materials or careless workmanship, not negligence by the home owner.

Under a new regulation, the FHA can repair severe defects if the builder is unable or unwilling to do it himself. This safeguard is effective up to four years, but only in new houses approved for FHA mortgages on or after September 2, 1964. To qualify, the structure must be "approved by FHA for a mortgage prior to the beginning of construction and inspected by FHA or VA during construction." Consult the FHA *before* buying a new house.

A used home bought with an FHA loan is not guaranteed against any defects. An FHA appraiser inspects the house in advance. If major defects are discovered, the FHA will insist that they be corrected before it will insure a mortgage. But flaws that develop after the new home owner moves in are his responsibility. The one exception to this regulation is a home that was originally constructed and bought as new with an FHA mortgage on or after September 2, 1964. In this case, the owner is protected up to four years after the dwelling was built.

Almost any home buyer is eligible for an FHA mortgage, provided he has a good credit record and enough cash for the down payment and closing costs. He must have a steady income large enough to meet the monthly mortgage payments without difficulty. No minimum income is set, but he must earn enough to buy a house at a given price. Nor does an inflexible age limit exist. The borrower's age and income are considered with other factors that enable FHA to decide whether he will be able to repay the loan.

The property must be acceptable by FHA minimum standards. Regardless of its price, an FHA spokesman said, "the dwelling must be well-planned, well-built, and located in a suitable neighborhood." A mortgage may be refused if the property is located in an area changing from residential to commercial and thus faces depreciating values.

An application can be made to any lending institution that has been approved by the FHA to make insured mortgage loans. If a loan is granted, the lender furnishes the necessary forms for the borrower to complete. These are then forwarded to the local FHA office for approval. If the house is part of a development, the builder will already have an FHA statement of the amount for which it will insure the structure.

THE VETERANS ADMINISTRATION (GI) LOAN

Loans are guaranteed by the VA to help veterans buy houses at reasonable terms. Private lending institutions are encouraged to give larger mortgages by the VA's guarantee that it will pay up to 60 percent of the loan if the borrower defaults. The maximum amount recoverable is $12,500. VA loans are granted for periods up to thirty years.

VA interest rates have risen with inflation and consequent scarcity of mortgage money. In the early 1950s, a VA loan was obtainable at 4 percent. By January 1970, the rate had risen to 8½ percent. The VA and FHA set their rates together. Although the VA imposes no charge for loans to World War II and Korean conflict veterans, post-Korean veterans must pay a fee of ½ of 1 percent on an insurance premium, raising their interest rate to 9 percent.

More than six million homes have been bought with VA loans since World War II. Eligibility for the majority of World War II veterans was supposed to expire July 25, 1967, but an amended law extended the expiration date to July 25, 1970. Applying this phase-out formula with generous flexibility, the VA will guarantee loans to the remaining eligible veterans. Korean conflict veterans' eligibility expires January 31, 1975. A veteran is defined as one who served in the Armed Forces for at least ninety days. Veterans of the Vietnam conflict are now included in this eligibility provision.

In 1965 the Housing and Urban Development Act devised a program for eligible veterans who had not availed themselves of a VA loan. These veterans are entitled to FHA insured mortgage loans, exempting them from a down payment on the first $15,000 of a home's value. For a house up to $25,000, 10 percent down payment is required, and 15 percent down payment on the value of a house over $25,000.

Veterans living in small towns or distant rural areas where mortgage money is not usually available at reasonable rates can receive loans directly from the VA. About ten thousand direct loans, up to

$17,500, are granted every year without a down payment. If a veteran wants to buy a more expensive house, he must pay the difference in cash.

VA loans can be made for the full amount of the appraised value. No down payment is necessary if the purchase price equals the appraised value. Veterans must make their own arrangements for a VA loan from private lending institutions. But the applicant is required to obtain a Certificate of Eligibility from the VA. If the property is a new house in a development, and the builder has made arrangements for VA loans, he will have the necessary forms to simplify the loan procedure.

DISCOUNTS OR POINTS

When mortgage money is "tight" or scarce, some lenders evade the FHA and VA maximum interest to fatten their profit margin through a procedure known as discounting: the borrower is charged a varying number of "points," each of which is 1 percent or one dollar for every hundred dollars of principal. For example, in return for a $20,000 FHA mortgage, the lender may demand five or more points. If the borrower agrees he is given only $19,000, which is $20,000 less 5 percent discounted in advance. But he will repay the full $20,000 loan. In tight money markets charges range up to ten points. The amount of the discount is supposed to equalize the disparity between the yield on FHA interest rates and the current return in the mortgage money market.

Builders who are compelled to pay points to make their homes eligible for FHA loans, simply add this cost to the price of their properties. Thus a builder may pay eight points so his house can be sold with a $20,000 FHA mortgage. Discounted in advance, the builder receives only $18,400; the difference or $1600 is pocketed by the lender.

It is an extremely rare builder who will absorb this cost himself. Some sell their houses on condition that the buyer defray this cost. Others recover this amount by cutting corners on materials or workmanship. Although prohibited by FHA regulations, discounts are ultimately shifted to the borrower. FHA rules, however, do not ban discount payments if the borrower is constructing a home for his own use or is refinancing an existing mortgage. Facing such extra charges, the alert borrower should shop for a mortgage lender who will provide loans in accordance with FHA regulations, or the fewest points possible.

THE CONVENTIONAL MORTGAGE

Any loan not guaranteed by the VA or insured by the FHA is known as conventional. The down payment on this kind of loan is usually higher than for a government-insured loan. At one time a dwelling could not be bought with a conventional loan unless the borrower paid at least one-third down; even 40 percent was not uncommon. Federal and state laws have now been amended, allowing smaller down payments and longer mortgage periods.

Mortgage terms are usually influenced by the amount of the down payment. Private lending institutions will often accept a lower interest rate with a larger down payment, if the mortgage amount is relatively low in relation to the property's value. Interest rates are traditionally higher in the West and lower in the East. Competing with each other for available mortgage money, lenders find that interest rates tend to be stable in any given area.

Private lending institutions are regulated by federal and state laws in the amount of money they may lend and the length of the mortgage. Most institutions will not lend the maximum allowed by law; the larger the down payment, the more secure is the mortgage. It is also advantageous for the borrower to give a large down payment, reducing his monthly installments. In any case, when money is plentiful the borrower has a better opportunity to receive a maximum loan.

Savings institutions form the largest pool of home mortgage lenders in the United States. Leading this group are *Savings and Loan Associations,* holding nearly 40 percent of all home mortgages. Savings and Loan Associations pioneered in amortized home loans years before other agencies adopted this sound practice.

Savings and Loan Associations are known in Louisiana as "Homestead Associations" and in Massachusetts as "Cooperative Banks." About 6,200 association offices are located throughout the country. Most are insured by the Federal Savings and Loan Insurance Corporation, a government agency. Well over 90 percent of their total assets are invested in home mortgages.

Leaning heavily toward conventional mortgages, these associations restrict loans largely to 66⅔ percent of appraised value. But they are legally allowed to grant 90 percent loans, meaning the down payment can be as low as 10 percent. In actual practice only a small number of such loans are given. New houses in highly desirable communities can often be bought with an 80 percent loan, that is, a 20 percent down payment. Shifting money demands greatly influence down payments.

Applied to all mortgage loans, these are specifically percentages of the *appraised* value, not the actual price paid for the house. Lenders are conservative, particularly those giving conventional loans. Their appraised value is almost unfailingly less than the actual amount paid for the property.

Life insurance companies hold about one-fifth of all the mortgage loans in the nation. Most of these lenders give mortgage loans through a bank, preferring not to deal directly with individuals. But a number of companies that deal directly with the home owner condition the loan on a "package" arrangement: the borrower is required to buy a life insurance policy to liquidate the mortgage loan, in the event that illness or death leaves his family without means to pay the installments. Although loans of the conventional type are preferred, life insurance companies do accept FHA and VA loans.

Mutual savings banks are located in eighteen states, largely in the middle Atlantic and New England areas. Most are in Massachusetts and New York State. More than 70 percent of mutual banks' assets are invested in mortgages, with the largest amounts in FHA and VA loans. Their loans range up to 80 percent of the appraised value, but member banks in New York State give up to 90 percent on conventional mortgages. These banks hold about 14 percent of all home mortgage loans.

Commercial banks are principally organized to accept demand deposits, known as checking accounts, allowing depositors to withdraw funds without notice or waiting time. They also perform a secondary function in accepting time deposits or savings accounts. Under their governing laws, banks accepting time deposits may stipulate that the depositor first give notice and then wait a specific period before withdrawing funds.

A Federal Reserve Act amendment in 1959 authorized national

banks to give loans on improved property up to 75 percent of its value provided full payment is made within twenty years. About 15 percent of home mortgage loans held by commercial banks are conventional, the rest are FHA and VA.

The Federal National Mortgage Association, also known as "Fanny May," authorized by Congress in 1938, was formed to buy FHA, later VA, mortgages from lenders in need of cash. It was a constructive Federal measure to increase the acceptability of FHA and VA mortgages. FNMA's funds are drawn from bond issues authorized by Congress.

Private mortgage firms and individual brokers act as agents for various lenders who seek first mortgages as a safe and secure investment. Some of these firms act exclusively for an insurance company, either as an agent or as a subsidiary. These brokers are a good source of FHA and VA loans.

As money becomes scarce some private lenders, looking ahead to the time when interest rates will be much higher, demand an unusual agreement by the borrower called an escalation clause. Almost invariably used in commercial office leasing, the escalation clause provides for increases to defray every tax increase, which is apportioned among all tenant firms on the basis of rentals. Referred to as *variable rate mortgages,* inclusion of this clause commits the borrower to pay his loan at a higher rate of interest to meet rising rates on the market. Home owners who accepted this condition at 6 percent are now paying mortgage installments at the rate of 9 percent. If interest rates should decline, which is not very likely, this clause would then benefit the borrower in some cases.

PURCHASE MONEY MORTGAGE

Sometimes the seller of a house may lend the buyer part of the purchase price, then take the mortgage himself as security. Known as a purchase money mortgage, this is often used in the purchase of an old house which is free and clear of any mortgage but on which a new mortgage would be very expensive. (The property may be in need of major repairs or over-valued.) As an inducement to the buyer, the seller accepts the mortgage himself. Some sellers offer this arrangement, then discount the purchase money mortgage by selling it to a mortgage firm or bank at a sum considerably lower than its face value.

Unless the buyer is knowledgeable in such matters, he should have the house appraised for its value and inspected for its condition. Lending agencies usually limit loans on an older house to a lower percentage of its appraised value than on a newer home.

But, assuming that the house is reasonably priced, a purchase money mortgage may be the only alternative open to a buyer. If the amount of a mortgage loan by a bank or other lender is far less than the price of the house, the seller may agree to a purchase mortgage for the difference. It also becomes a second mortgage which bears higher interest rates.

AN EXISTING MORTGAGE

A house sold with an option to assume the owner's mortgage usually has a lower interest rate. Many homes bought in the past decade or two carry thirty-year mortgages with interest rates ranging from 4½ percent to 5 percent, much lower than current interest rates. Although money saved in this manner could be substantial, accepting such a mortgage requires a higher down payment, because the seller must recover his investment in one lump sum.

FAVORABLE MORTGAGE FEATURES

Prepayment privileges are contained in all VA and FHA mortgages, permitting the borrower to prepay part or all of his loan before the mortgage is due. Conventional mortgages usually impose a penalty for prepayments, requiring the borrower to pay an additional charge. As the inflationary spiral forces interest rates up, more lenders include prepayment clauses without penalty. Confident that rates will continue to rise, they prefer prepayment of loans at 5½ percent so that they can lend this money to a new borrower at 9 percent or more.

An open-end mortgage permits the home owner to borrow money at a future date, avoiding additional high closing costs. Such a loan usually does not exceed the amount already paid on the mortgage.

If after a given number of years, for example, $10,000 has been paid, the owner would have no difficulty borrowing $9,000 for major alterations. Sometimes such a loan can be secured at the original rate of interest.

A package mortgage enables the borrower to include the cost of major appliances, storm windows, carpeting, and other essential household items. Such expenditures are added to the mortgage loan, payable at the same interest rate for the same length of time. This clause appeals to the buyer with a limited budget who moves into a new or otherwise partially equipped home.

The loan modification clause permits flexibility in payments if illness or death interrupts the family's normal income. Provisions arrange for skipped payments that extend beyond the expiration date of the mortgage. Some lenders, notably insurance companies, combine a mortgage loan with a life insurance policy on the borrower. Part of the payments are used to accumulate a fund against which the family in crisis can borrow to continue mortgage installments. After a given number of years, this fund may be sufficient to apply toward mortgage installments for many months.

Every mortgage specifies the exact amount lent to the borrower and the monthly sums toward repayment. The interest rate is clearly set forth. Interest rates, governed by state laws, currently range from 7½ percent in the East to 8 percent or higher in the West. A lender who charges more interest than that allowed by law is guilty of usury and may be barred from regaining his loan and interest due. Lenders may adjust the difference by charging points or discounts, without violating the statutes. In all states, however, a corporate borrower (business firm) may pay any rate set by the lender. Laws against usury apply only to individual borrowers.

ESCROW ACCOUNT

Many lending institutions set up an escrow account for the new home owner whereby funds are accumulated to pay his real estate taxes and fire insurance premiums. This money is apportioned and added to the monthly payments on the mortgage loan. Some lenders avoid this additional bookkeeping chore by having the home owner pay these sums directly.

Families on close budgets will find the escrow account financially convenient. Unexpected expenses may force them to borrow at a higher rate of interest to meet their tax bill or insurance premium when due. It is preferable that the lender make these payments through an escrow account.

TRUTH-IN-LENDING LAW

All credit transactions are governed by the Consumer Credit Protection Act, popularly called truth-in-lending, enacted by Congress July 1, 1969. The law does not limit amounts paid for credit, but it requires all who give credit to furnish a detailed and accurate description of all yearly finance charges, or "annual percentage rate" for each hundred dollars of unpaid balance.

Applied to real estate loans, the lender must reveal the yearly percentage rate and finance charge for each hundred dollars. These include such charges as points and insurance premiums for mortgage loans with some exceptions.

When you borrow to buy or build a house, the lending agency is not required to show the total interest cost of the loan. In this matter, Congress compromised with lending institutions and the real estate industry, which view such disclosures with alarm. They fear that many prospective home buyers might back away if shown the total interest charge over the life of the loan. (See Mortgage Payment Table, p. 177.) But the lender must list the yearly finance charge or percentage rate for each hundred dollars.

In computing the yearly percentage rate, lenders are not compelled to include fees or premiums for title examination, title insurance, fees for preparing a deed or settlement statement, fees for notarizing deeds and other documents, fees for credit reports and appraisal, and charges for sums placed in escrow for future payment of insurance, taxes, sewer, and water assessments.

A provision designed to protect the home owner against a potentially ruinous second mortgage or lien gives him the legal right to cancel any contract, except a first mortgage, at will within three business days after the lender or contractor supplies the information demanded by law, including a detailed list of interest rates and other finance charges that were previously concealed from the borrower.

When a contractor offers an agreement permitting him to place a mechanic's lien on a house or a bill to be paid in more than four installments, he must give the owner two copies of a special form that enumerates the latter's rights. The owner may cancel the contract within the prescribed three business days merely by signing one copy and mailing it to the contractor. The agreement may also be rescinded by telegram.

Within ten days after receipt of the cancellation notice, the contractor must return any deposit or down payment. He may not deduct even one dollar for alleged expenses. Bound by the same terms, the contractor cannot begin work until the three-day cancellation period ends. Should an emergency require immediate attention, the home owner must waive his cancellation right in a signed statement.

Lenders and contractors who violate this law are subject to prosecution by the federal government. The home owner also has the right to sue for twice the amount of a finance charge, if the sum is not less than $100 or more than $1,000. If the owner wins, the lender or contractor must pay an equitable fee to the former's lawyer and all court costs.

You can protect yourself in most transactions by noting the annual amount of finance charges or interest rates for each $100. Be sure you completely understand the contract before signing it.

This new bill of rights for the home owner and consumer will have far-reaching effects. Under terms of the act, the federal government will cede enforcement power to individual states as they enact laws fully consistent with the Consumer Credit Protection Act.

THE SECOND MORTGAGE

Second mortgages are shunned by the VA, FHA, and lending institutions governed by federal and state laws because a second mortgage poses a much greater risk than a first lien. In the event of foreclosure, proceeds from the sale are used to pay the first loan. Rarely is any money left to repay the holder of the second mortgage. Private lenders are the only source of second mortgages. Some are reliable; many are not.

A second mortgage is the home owner's flag of distress. He has already borrowed above and beyond the amount owed on the first loan. Risking loss of their investment, private lenders exact proportionately high payments. Many second mortgage operators lure distressed home owners through enticing newspaper ads, only to entrap them into paying exorbitant charges.

Denouncing schemes that offer distressed home owners a seemingly easy way to reduce the amount of their monthly payments, the Better Business Bureau warned that this operation "is spreading like wildfire throughout the United States and Canada."

Frantically clutching at any means to pay pressing creditors, home owners eagerly respond to such ads as this: "Home owner loans . . . Need $2,000 or more? Repay only $35 monthly including interest . . . Let us show you how to pay off everything you owe . . ." Often, only a post office box is listed, or a telephone number which is an answering service.

Told that the interest is no higher than the prevailing legal rate, the borrower places a second mortgage on his home, the loan to be paid in three to five years. Signing without further investigation is the first misstep in a costly blunder. A careful reading of the contract would suggest that, in trying to liquidate onerous debts, the borrower is loading himself with a far more oppressive obligation.

Most of the second mortgage usurers are not licensed as real estate brokers or money lenders and regrettably are exempt from laws in many states. One of the few exceptions is the Wisconsin Banking Department, which has ruled that charging a brokerage fee beside the maximum interest rate is illegal under Wisconsin statutes.

Shortly after signing the contract, the borrower is saddled with miscellaneous fees. Citing the case of an Ohio woman who borrowed $3,000 on a second mortgage, the Better Business Bureau reported that she learned her debt amounted to $5,850 over a five year period, payable at $97.50 a month, almost double the amount of her loan.

At times a second mortgage may be desirable, when an individual lacks all the cash necessary for a down payment. If a buyer of a $25,000 home, for example, is unable to obtain a mortgage higher than $15,000 but has only $4,000 in cash, he may consider a second mortgage of $6,000. But the interest rate will reflect the high risk.

Anyone offered a second mortgage loan on an easy three to five year plan should think hard and long before gulping the bait. A harried debtor is well advised to seek advice from the lending institution that has the first mortgage. The Better Business Bureau will be helpful in screening the most voracious usurers. More important, the home owner should not sign any contract unless it is completely understood.

HOW TO OBTAIN YOUR MORTGAGE

Obtaining a mortgage loan begins with filling out an application form prepared by the lending agency. Besides describing the property and its location, the applicant lists his employment, income, assets, and debts. He also authorizes the lender to examine his bank account. A copy of the sales contract must accompany the application. In special cases, the lender will ask for plans and specifications of the property.

A credit investigation is initiated to confirm the applicant's information and his eligibility for the loan; this is usually a routine matter. A favorable credit report is followed by an appraiser's evaluation of the property. Because the lender gives a loan on a percentage of the appraised value and not the actual price paid, the appraiser's observations are in line with his employer's policy. He will intentionally underestimate its value. Thus a house costing $30,000 may be appraised at $25,000, on which the applicant receives a 70 percent mortgage or $17,500. If the borrower defaults in his payments, the lender's investment would not be endangered in the slightest.

A survey of the property is made to determine whether the structure encroaches on adjoining property or violates a zoning ordinance or building code. Since these conditions could render the home unsalable, the loan will probably be denied. Although the borrower pays for the survey, and other expenses, discovery of one or more violations is ultimately in his interest.

If the lender approves the application, the buyer is notified by a *letter of commitment,* which amounts to a guarantee that he will receive the loan in the amount requested. He must respond in writing within a specified time—about two weeks—accepting the lender's terms, or his application will be discarded. Applications for conventional mortgages bring quicker approval than those for FHA and VA loans. Loans from the governmental agencies require more time for processing.

A title search is then ordered, either by the borrower or lender. If the title is free of defects or flaws, the borrower buys a title insurance policy to protect the lender's investment against possible claims until the loan is paid in full.

The mortgage table shows monthly payments on principal and interest for each one-thousand dollar loan. Not included are amounts for other items, such as taxes, property insurance, and special assessments which vary in different localities.

To find the cost of a $15,000 mortgage, for example, at 7½ percent interest for 30 years: follow the line of interest rate to column under time of loan (thirty years) to the figure $7.00; multiply this figure by the amount of loan (15,000) in thousand dollar units (15) to show the monthly payment of $105.00; multiply the monthly payment by 12 (months) to show the yearly payment of $1,260.00; multiply the yearly payment by time of loan (30 years) to show the total cost of $37,800; deduct the principal ($15,000) from the total amount to show the interest paid of $22,800.

MORTGAGE TABLE

TABLE 9

MONTHLY PAYMENTS TO AMORTIZE EACH $1,000 OF LOAN

	Time of Loan					
% Interest	10 Yrs.	15 Yrs.	20 Yrs.	25 Yrs.	30 Yrs.	35 Yrs.
5¼	10.73	8.04	6.74	6.00	5.53	5.21
5½	10.85	8.17	6.89	6.15	5.68	5.37
5¾	10.98	8.31	7.03	6.30	5.84	5.54
6	11.11	8.44	7.17	6.45	6.00	5.71
6¼	11.23	8.58	7.31	6.60	6.16	5.88
6½	11.36	8.72	7.46	6.76	6.33	6.05
6¾	11.49	8.85	7.61	6.91	6.49	6.22
7	11.62	8.99	7.76	7.07	6.66	6.39
7¼	11.75	9.13	7.91	7.23	6.83	6.57
7½	11.88	9.28	8.06	7.39	7.00	6.75
7¾	12.01	9.42	8.21	7.56	7.17	6.93
8	12.14	9.56	8.37	7.72	7.34	7.11
8¼	12.27	9.70	8.53	7.88	7.51	7.29
8½	12.40	9.84	8.69	8.04	7.68	7.47
8¾	12.53	9.98	8.85	8.20	7.85	7.65
9	12.66	10.12	9.01	8.36	8.02	7.83
9¼	12.79	10.26	9.17	8.52	8.19	8.01
9½	12.92	10.40	9.33	8.68	8.36	8.19
9¾	13.05	10.54	9.49	8.84	8.53	8.37
10	13.18	10.68	9.65	9.00	8.70	8.55

Chapter 16

Other Legal Considerations

Too often a prospective buyer fails to grasp the relatively high cost of home ownership, especially in the initial period. Mortgage payments are the largest monthly expense, but other expenditures must be considered.

THE BINDER

After agreeing on a price, the buyer and seller may sign a *binder* in which the former gives a deposit as evidence of his serious intention to buy. If a broker is involved, he arranges the binder. Depending upon its wording, a binder may or may not have the force of a contract. More frequently, it is a temporary agreement to bind the parties until a formal contract is drawn, usually by the seller's attorney. Deposits may range from $50 to $1,000, based on the sale price of the house.

In many instances the broker or seller will refuse to return binder money if the buyer changes his mind. You can protect yourself against such a loss by including a provision that the money is returnable at your request in a certain number of days. During that time you can carefully inspect the property or have a professional house inspector examine the house and garage. Still better, anyone who has advanced this far in buying a house should have a competent attorney to guide him.

THE CONTRACT OF SALE

The contract of sale, known variously as a sales contract, conditional sales contract, or purchase contract, is the first legally binding step toward the purchase of a house. The signing of a contract of sale is accompanied by a deposit, usually 10 percent of the price, paid to the seller. This money is not returnable should the buyer withdraw after the contract has been signed. If a lending institution's appraiser discovers a major structural defect, a badly fractured foundation, for example, it will refuse the loan. Unless the buyer is protected in the contract, he will be poorer by the amount of his deposit.

A protective clause may read: "This contract of sale is conditioned upon the ability of the buyer to obtain a mortgage in the sum of $25,000 for a period of 25 to 30 years at the prevailing rate of interest at the time of the closing of the title." Should the seller decide to withdraw from the deal, the buyer may agree or not, as he chooses. He can compel the seller to fulfill his agreement by court action.

Another protective measure is to assure the prompt refund of your deposit if the house is destroyed by fire, or any other disaster, after the contract is signed but before the title is closed. If the money is paid directly to the seller, he may be unable or unwilling to return it. By placing the deposit in escrow with your lawyer or a bank (which may be the lender) you can avoid a potentially expensive and troublesome problem.

This may not always be easy. A seller may need your deposit for a down payment on a house he plans to buy. Another potential problem arises when the seller is a builder from whom you are buying a house still unbuilt. Since a builder often operates on a narrow financial margin, he will most likely demand the money to pay his construction costs. Should he become bankrupt when only the foundation for your house has been laid, you face the loss of your money. Only you can decide whether to chance such risks.

During inflationary periods, real property is generally sold at a higher price than the owner paid. At the time ownership is transferred, the lender usually requires additional fire insurance to meet the purchase price. If the mortgagee, for any reason, fails to request such adjustment, it is important that you arrange for increased coverage to correspond to the property's value.

Refuse to sign a contract if the seller insists that the closing date be held in abeyance until his housing needs are satisfactorily met. Should he be unable to buy another house or encounter delay in occupancy, you and your family may be forced to live expensively in a hotel or motel for weeks, perhaps months. Insist upon ownership and occupancy on the same date.

The sale of real estate does not include personal things (chattel) unless these are specifically mentioned in the contract. Personal property comprises stoves, refrigerators, washers and dryers, carpets, draperies, garden tools, and fixtures that can be removed without considerable damage to ceilings or walls.

Printed contract forms usually contain a section listing personal property included in the sale, such as stoves, refrigerators, and similar personal items. Where no provision is made for certain articles, these can then be listed under a clause that may read, "In addition to the personal property described above, the folllowing personal property items are also included in this contract of sale." When listing major appliances, be sure to include the manufacturer's name, model number, and capacity or size.

If the buyer agrees to purchase any other personal property, this should be similarly itemized and described, including the price of each, in a separate statement (bill of sale) signed by the seller.

TITLE INSURANCE

After the bank is notified by the borrower that he will accept the loan, a title search is begun on the property to reveal whatever legal defects exist. The seller's deed of sale does not guarantee the buyer against legal claims that may date several generations back. A title search is an examination of all recorded documents that affect ownership of the property.

Although such a search may disclose nothing suspicious, it is inadequate protection against hitherto undetected title defects. This is why lenders require title insurance by the buyer to defray costs stemming from the defense of title, and to pay claims if necessary.

Forgery on deeds is not uncommon. Skillful falsifiers have clouded title to thousands of homes. Forgeries are perpetrated by the most unlikely people, which explains why the fraud continues undetected for many years. The culprit may be the seemingly gentle person who actually is a disgruntled spouse and forges his or her name to a deed. Such crimes have often occurred several generations back, involving people utterly unknown to the buyer or seller. But a forged deed conveys no valid title to property.

Vague or improperly drawn wills plague many innocent buyers of real estate. Thus a person believed to be without living kin dies, and his property is disposed of in a presumably legal manner. Years later missing relatives may appear to demand their share of the property from the new owner who believes he possesses it legally.

If a search discloses no discernible defects, the title insurance company will issue a policy agreeing to insure the buyer's title. Should any legal action be initiated against the buyer, the title insurance company will defend him at its expense. If the title proves defective, resulting in the loss of the property, the title company will reimburse the home owner in full for the amount of the title insurance. The premium for such a policy is generally ½ to 1 percent of the sale price. It is paid by the buyer only once, at the time it is issued.

DEEDS

A valid deed is evidence of real estate ownership and usually is acquired by purchase or inheritance. Every proper contract specifies the type of deed to be given. Since the rights of both parties are incontestably fixed by terms of the contract, which is drawn by the seller's lawyer, the buyer is best served by his own professional adviser.

All deed forms begin with "This Indenture," a term that has no legal significance today. It originated in early English law when a deed was torn in two, half retained by the seller and half by the buyer. Any subsequent dispute about the document's validity was quickly settled by fitting together the indented edges of the two parts.

Among the most common forms of deed, the *full covenant and warranty deed* offers the greatest protection. It is the seller's guarantee against such defects in title as liens and encumbrances. If any are found after the closing, the seller is obligated to compensate the buyer for any loss. Most sellers decline to give this type of deed, not because they necessarily have defective titles, but are reluctant to be saddled with a potential burden after disposing of their property. In the rare cases when such a deed is granted, it should not be misconstrued as a safe substitute for title insurance.

A *bargain and sale deed with covenants* is the seller's assurance that during his ownership he caused no title defect. But he disclaims all responsibility for encumbrances and liens brought about by previous owners. This type of deed, the most frequently given, is comparable to the *special warranty deed* which is used in some states.

A *quitclaim deed* is often used to correct title defects as they appear in the public record. Sometimes it is given by persons to quit a claim through inheritance. Without guarantee or assurance to the new owner, it conveys only whatever interest the seller has in the property. A buyer who accepts a quitclaim deed on property later revealed to be heavily impaired by liens and encumbrances is liable for these debts. By accepting a quitclaim deed, he has forfeited his right to recover losses from the previous owner.

Formal stipulations for a binding deed are not uniform in every state, but certain requirements are commonly shared. The seller's name should be spelled as it appears on his deed. If the property is owned by two or more persons, their names are to be listed as sellers. No variation in name or spelling of name is permitted on the deed.

If married, the same importance attaches to the name of the buyer and his wife. By listing "John Smith and Mary Smith, his wife," a *tenancy by the entirety* arises. Neither one can sell his or her interest without the other's agreement. Upon the death of either, the survivor automatically becomes the sole owner of the property.

The actual purchase price need not be mentioned except in those states where mandatory. Elsewhere the words "in consideration of one dollar and other good and sufficient consideration" are usually substituted to prevent any future buyer from knowing the full purchase price. But the cost can be learned from the amount of Federal tax stamps affixed to the deed (see page 217).

Description of the property should be identical to that in the contract, which is checked against the seller's deed. Most real estate transactions on the same property repeatedly describe the boundaries without any change. Each new description should be checked against the latest survey.

All restrictions and conditions included in the contract belong in the deed. If the property is sold subject to a mortgage, the type, amount, and unpaid balance are to be listed. In signing the deed, the seller is expected to write his name exactly as it is spelled elsewhere in the form. The buyer also signs in the same manner.

Some states require the deed to be witnessed by one or two persons to be eligible for recording, but witnesses are not necessary in other areas. Most states require a deed be acknowledged before a notary public. The seller appears before this public officer who acknowledges that the vendor voluntarily signed the deed.

Recording a deed is the final act after closing. All states have enacted laws to establish a permanent public record of real property titles. Every new owner of property should record his deed with a designated officer in the county where the real estate is located. Titles of these officers vary in different states but their functions are the same. They are most frequently known as the registrar of deeds, the county recorder, or the county clerk.

Time and again buyers who neglected to record deeds have found themselves in a financial nightmare. A dishonest owner, who learns that the buyer has neglected to record the deed, may resell the property to an unsuspecting person. For example, A sold a parcel of land to B and gave him a good signed deed. Neglecting to record the document, B placed it in his file. Upon learning of B's imprudence, A resold the property to C, who promptly recorded it, notifying the public of his ownership.

Later, when B attempted to sell the property, his buyer searched the public record only to find it was actually owned by C. In the ensuing lawsuit and appeal, the courts ruled that the property belonged to C. B's unrecorded deed was not worth the paper on which it was written. Jailing A for fraud was scant comfort. Record your deed promptly and be secure.

Some states (California, Colorado, Washington, D.C., Delaware, Mississippi, Missouri, Tennessee, Texas, Virginia, West Virginia) substitute the *deed of trust* for a mortgage. The borrower deeds his property to a trustee, or third party, in behalf of the lender. Held as security until the loan is repaid, the trustee then deeds the property back to the borrower. If payments are not made, the trustee can deed the property to the lender or dispose of it by auction, depending on the individual state's law.

CLOSING COSTS

Mortgage lenders, whether they are banks or insurance companies, require the buyer to pay the difference between the purchase price and the amount of the mortgage loan as a down payment. If, for example, you buy a house for $30,000 and are given a $20,000 mortgage, the lender requires a down payment of $10,000.

When the deed transfers ownership of the property from seller to buyer, title is *closed*. Other initial expenses are the various closing costs at this time. Closing fees, also known as settlement charges, seldom are less than $400; they range as high as $1,200. Builders who offer their houses with "no closing costs" often thrive on this deception because some new home buyers are unaware of closing costs. The sellers simply add $500 or more to the purchase price of the house. Some builders frankly state that closing costs are included in the purchase price.

No home buyer can obtain a mortgage without paying settlement costs, usually by certified check, at the closing. These amounts vary among lending agencies, depending upon whether the house is new or used, and whether the buyer retains an existing mortgage or assumes a new one.

There have been numerous cases of excessive closing fees charged by grasping lenders. By the time a buyer receives a letter of commitment from the lender, the latter can estimate with fair accuracy the amount of closing costs. But too many lenders turn the closing into a fleecing session with the buyer as the sheep. If the real estate agent arranged the loan, his "finder's fee" will be added to the costs but concealed from the buyer. It may be included under some nebulous item, such as "service charge." Your best protection is an alert real estate lawyer who will provide for the return of your down payment and withdrawal from the deal if closing costs exceed an agreed-upon equitable amount.

A list of typical closing fees for a $15,000 mortgage is given in Table 10.

TABLE 10

Origination Fee *	$150.00
Title Search and Insurance	130.00
Survey of Property	50.00
Mortgage Application	9.00
Recording Deed	6.00
Mortgage Tax	75.00
Legal Fee to Lender's Attorney	100.00
Appraisal Fee	35.00
Credit Report on Borrower	5.00
Total:	$560.00

* Origination fee, also known as mortgage service charge, is paid to the lender for granting the loan, processing it, and other assorted smaller services. Both VA and FHA limit this fee to 1 percent. It may be higher in conventional mortgages.

Additional costs paid at the closing are adjustments apportioned between buyer and seller. These are fire insurance, local taxes, fuel costs, and creation of an escrow account. Your share will be computed by your lawyer (whose fee should be included in your estimate of your initial costs).

Chapter 17

Other Home Ownership Expenses

MOVING

Moving companies that transport household goods across state lines are regulated by the Interstate Commerce Commission (ICC), a federal government agency. Moves within the same state are regulated under state law, if at all. Many rules have been issued for the benefit of shippers or customers, but the ICC cannot protect the indifferent householder against overcharge by unconscionable carriers. Whether you pay fair charges depends how clearly you understand the terms and conditions of the contract.

Moving costs are based on the actual total weight of the shipment, which is determined by weighing the van before and after it is loaded. The difference is the net weight of the household goods. When the mover visits your home, he makes a rough estimate of the weight of the possessions you will ship and gives you an estimated price. This is not a guaranteed price. You will learn the full cost after the goods have been removed, but before they are delivered, because the van is weighed after loading. ICC regulations do not hold a mover to his estimate, but if the estimate is wrong by more than 10 percent or twenty-five dollars, whichever is greater, ICC regulations require him to notify you at least twenty-four hours before delivery. You are in effect cautioned to have enough money if the charges are higher than the estimate.

Some movers deliberately submit an estimate so low as to suggest they made a "mistake" in favor of the shipper. By the time of delivery, however, the customer is compelled to pay the charges even if they are twice the estimate. Deception is not practiced by falsifying the weight, but by intentionally under-estimating it when the goods are checked in the customer's home.

Total moving costs are determined by multiplying the actual weight of the shipment by the carrier's rate which is based on distance in mileage. For example, a 7,000 pound load moved 600 miles at $8 for each 100 pounds would amount to $560. Rates, called tariffs, are published in book form, along with charges and rules of the carriers, and must be used in computing the amount on a shipment.

Every carrier whom you contact for an estimate is required by the ICC to give you a printed statement entitled *Important Notice to Shippers of Household Goods*. It contains information on estimates, carrier responsibility, notification of charges and delay, payment and delivery, and lost or damaged articles. A carrier who consistently neglects to provide this statement is subject to prosecution. If a van agent fails to give you this notice, think twice before signing a contract with him.

Charges for local moving are based on hourly rates. Multiplying the rate by the number of hours determines the total cost. But the shipper must make additional payments for special optional services performed by the carrier, such as packing, unpacking, appliance servicing, etc.

Moving companies cannot prosper if they continually cheat the public. Obtain estimates from four or five carriers. Ask each for the names of several customers whose goods were moved to your city or community. Check with them as well as the Better Business Bureau. If a mover declines to give you names for reference, he has already told you much about himself.

Other carriers to be avoided are those who hint that ICC regulations set the same rates for all movers. Each carrier may charge what he pleases, but must file his rates with the government's regulatory body. All moving companies are required to show their published rates at your request.

Moving Insurance

Steer clear of the mover who assures you his firm is "fully insured" or "bonded." Such claims are worthless and are intended to dupe the incautious customer. Unless the customer arranges for full value protection, a carrier's liability for goods damaged in transit is limited to 60¢ a pound. Thus if a $370 portable color TV set weighing 55 pounds is damaged beyond repair, the customer will receive only $33.

Carriers are very reluctant to move jewelry, money, negotiable bonds, securities, and similar valuables. Nor will a prudent customer include these in his shipment. If you insist, do not fail to declare these for full value protection. A carrier's liability for uninsured lost valuables is also limited to 60¢ for each pound.

When a costly painting is to be shipped, the van line requires that it be examined by a recognized art expert and insured at its appraised value. Objects of art and coin or stamp collections must also be submitted for expert appraisal. These must be packed by the mover at extra cost for the insurance to remain in force.

If you intend to do your own packing, read the agreement carefully. Regardless of insurance, most contracts protect the mover against liability for damaged fragile items, such as china and glassware, if the customer packed these himself. But the carrier is fully responsible for such damage caused by negligent employees as dented or chipped plaster, broken windows, or a trampled flower bed. Such claims are usually settled without demur if the company is notified promptly in writing.

Upon signing an agreement with a mover, you should be given an inventory form to list all goods. This is important because it will protect you against loss or damage. By checking each item as it is loaded, and again when unloaded, you can note its condition. If all goods are delivered in the same condition as when shipped, your signature confirms this.

Any damage or loss should be noted on the form, and is your record for claims. It may take considerable time to carefully check your goods; pay no heed to an impatient van driver who tries to hurry you. The terms of the agreement should require him to join you in checking the goods. Since all claims must be based on this record, be sure every item is inspected before signing the form. It is unlikely you will collect for an expensive phonograph if you discover the damage after the van men leave with the signed form.

Reputable movers will provide an "estimated cost of service form" in writing. You can help by not overlooking heavy, bulky items stored in the attic or garage. This is a good opportunity to dispose of useless articles. String-saving habits at such a time can be expensive in space, work, and money. Old magazines, papers, books, excess furniture, and worn clothing you "may" use some day should be given to a worthwhile charitable agency. Remember, it may cost more to move an old, well-used lawn mower than its actual worth.

Including flammable items in the shipment could be a costly blunder. Public carriers are forbidden to transport such hazardous material. In case of fire, the customer may be denied any claim resulting from his negligence. Drain the gas tanks and oil reservoirs of lawn mowers and gasoline-powered tools. Discard acids and other dangerous liquids and articles that may damage clothing, furnishings, or furniture.

Draw a floor plan of your new home, indicating where furniture and other articles are to be placed, and give the van men a copy. Place corresponding signs outside each room. Label every carton, barrel, and crate so they may be easily identified and placed in the room where you want them. All items not to be moved should be separated and assembled in one place; call the mover's attention to these. Plane or railroad tickets should not be placed in furniture drawers. You may give them no thought until the packed van is on its way. It has happened many times before.

Extra Moving Charges

Special services, other than transportation, are performed at additional cost. For example, the carrier will pack or unpack all or part of your goods as you choose, for an additional fee. But the company reserves the right to re-pack fragile articles that are improperly crated, boxed, or packed, at an extra charge.

A refrigerator, stove, washing machine, or other heavy appliance that requires special servicing, including disconnection, before moving will be handled at an additional charge. Unless you take down window cornices, draperies, blinds, mirrors, and other articles attached to walls, or pick up tacked down rugs, the mover will do this and add charges for these services.

Exclusive use of the mover's vehicle also means an additional charge. An interstate carrier can transport your property with that of others in the same van. At your request, a van will be provided solely for your goods at a much higher rate. Van lines are usually not required to deliver on a certain date or within a given period. Excessively delayed deliveries cause the largest number of complaints to the ICC. Expedited service is available, meaning your shipment will arrive on a specified date, also at a higher cost.

Storage in transit provides for your property to be stored and delivered at a later date. Failure to give the van line final instructions will result in permanent storage, ending the carrier's liability. Your goods will be released only on payment of all warehouse costs, plus a charge for moving the property out of storage.

An interstate carrier will not deliver or relinquish any articles of a personal shipment until all charges have been paid in cash, certified check, money order, or traveler's checks. Since your personal check will be refused, be sure you have payment in one of the acceptable forms. Otherwise, the mover may put your shipment in transit storage at a minimum thirty-day charge, including the cost of moving it from warehouse back to your dwelling after you pay. If the moving men are kept waiting while you raise the money, you will be further charged the full hourly rate for each man assigned to the vehicle. Other arrangements can be made in cases of company moves, or if you establish credit with the carrier.

When paying charges get a receipt for the amount paid, specifying the gross (van + goods) and tare (goods only) weights of the vehicle and the net weight of your goods, the mileage, the applicable rate for each hundred pounds, transportation charges, additional insurance, and any special services performed. The receipt is called a freight bill or expense bill.

All claims for loss or damage must be filed in writing with the carrier, who is subject to ICC rules and regulations. However, the ICC is not empowered to compel the van line to settle claims. Nor can it rule whether the company is liable. If the mover refuses to pay such claims, the customer's only recourse is to file a suit in a court of law. By clearly understanding your rights and obligations, you can avoid a costly and vexatious lawsuit.

PAINTING AND DECORATING

Any initial allowance for painting and decorating depends on the house selected. If you buy a new home, exterior painting will not be necessary unless you prefer a color that is not included in the builder's offer. Interiors of most new homes are finished in neutral shades. If you choose a house from plans or before it is completed, you will be given a limited choice of paint colors. If these are not satisfactory, a change will be made at additional cost.

A well-maintained older home may not require exterior painting, or it may be built of masonry materials. Cement stucco does not require painting but some new home owners have it painted under the impression it is "dirty"—an unnecessary cost. Once a stucco house is painted, it will require paint maintenance just as any other painted house.

If the home's interior requires painting, or if you want to change colors, this is most conveniently done before you move in. Get several estimates as you would for any other work. Painting costs are higher during the peak seasons of spring, summer, and early fall than during the slow seasons of late autumn and winter.

You can specify the brand and type of paint that you want. Paint prices are generally uniform for those of similar quality, but some unscrupulous painters may charge you extra for the brand you name. You can forestall this gouge by checking paint prices in advance.

In recent years durable, water-thinned paints have become available in a wide variety of colors. Acrylic latex, one of the best, is made for exterior and interior use. It can be applied smoothly with roller or brush, even on damp walls, and dries quickly in an odorless, tough finish. Acrylic latex spills are easily wiped clean with a sponge or cloth moistened with water. Rollers and brushes are easily cleaned in soapy water. For this reason, many home owners now do their own interior painting.

Storm doors and windows are now more commonly seen on used homes and are almost always extra in new houses. Their cost may be included in your mortgage. Since new homes are not equipped with shades or blinds, these will also be an additional expense.

Nearly all moves entail the cost of some new furniture and household equipment. Some purchases may be postponed but others must be immediate, such as new beds for children who acquire their own rooms.

A move to another state or area where you are unknown may require the posting of a deposit with the telephone and the utility companies. Such miscellaneous household and equipment expenses vary with each family's particular needs. An allowance of 5 percent of the home's price should adequately cover such expenditures.

LANDSCAPING

Model houses may be artistically landscaped, but this improvement usually is not part of your home's price. Grounds of most new houses are generally barren of trees and shrubs; the only shade is that provided by the house. Perhaps your only landscaping will be a rye grass lawn sown by the builder after the bulldozer left. Rye grass produces a fast-growing green lawn which is only temporary.

Many county agricultural agents, local botanical gardens, and nurserymen are excellent sources for expert guidance in planning your garden. The shrubbery and plants used will depend on the part of the country in which you live. Plants that thrive in California will not be suited to New England's climate; only plants native to a specific area are best.

A frequent tendency in landscaping new houses is to use too many shrubs and plants. Since these are small when bought, they may appear inadequate but will grow rapidly. Barren spaces should be filled with quick-growing, colorful annuals that are available at the local nursery or supermarket. You can also grow them from seed.

For an "instant" colorful garden, generous use of zinnias, marigolds, and petunias, three hardy annuals, has proved popular with numerous home owners. These inexpensive flowers can be grown from seed and will often reseed themselves for another year of bloom.

Extensive use of annuals is not satisfactory for long-term garden planning, because these plants grow, bloom, and fade in one year and require replacement. Perennials are more desirable since they reappear year after year and respond with colorful bloom to little care.

Gardens in older homes may be overgrown or overcrowded. In such cases, leave landscaping plans until the next growing season, if possible. This will give you an opportunity to see the garden in bloom and then to decide how and if you want to change it.

Since it frequently takes several years for shrubs and trees to become established, you should buy these plants from a nursery that guarantees them as healthy and will replace any that are unsatisfactory within a specified time. For an extra charge, nurserymen will prepare the soil and place your shrubs and trees to assure proper planting.

If you intend to have your grounds maintained by professional gardeners, give first consideration to those who work in your neighborhood and then compare their estimates. Prices are based on general lawn care, clean-up and maintenance of borders, and sweeping sidewalks. Extra charges are made for spring and fall clean-ups, and such items as hedge-clipping, pruning, and spraying trees.

Chapter 18

Recurrent Costs

Future costs of home ownership require the new owner to estimate all recurrent expenses carefully.

MORTGAGE PAYMENTS

The full amounts of the loan and interest are added together and then divided into equal monthly payments. Each remittance reduces part of the principal and part of the interest. Payments in the early years are applied mostly to interest and in later years largely reduce or amortize the principal. If an escrow account has been established, the amount of the monthly mortgage payment does not remain fixed. An increase in taxes or fire insurance rates, for example, may result in a new monthly rate, which is usually established annually by the lending institution.

TAXES

Real estate taxes represent the greatest single source of support to schools and municipal services. The tax rates vary in different areas. If you move into a newly developed community which has neither schools nor sewers, a steep tax rise is inevitable. To prevent foreclosure on your home for failure to pay taxes, the mortgage institution may require an escrow account from which it will pay your taxes and insurance.

INSURANCE

The lending bank, also interested in protecting its loan, obliges the owner to carry adequate fire insurance. The cost of premiums is often held in the escrow account and becomes part of your monthly payment. Life insurance premiums of ½ of 1 percent on FHA and some VA loans are also added. If you have one of the package deals requiring life insurance, the premium for this policy will also be part of the recurring costs.

Three types of insurance are essential to the home owner: fire, theft, and personal liability. Coverage within these groups ranges from minimal to comprehensive and embodies numerous related risks. Since many home owners are already insured against fire and burglary on personal property, these expenses will not be new. Most householders, however, underestimate the amount of fire insurance for their furnishings.

Personal liability insurance is needed by the home owner to cover his legal responsibility for accidental injury, or for damage to others' property that may occur on his premises. Package protection for home owners includes various forms of fire, burglary, and personal liability insurance in one policy, at one premium, with one expiration date. Mortgage disability insurance is an extra protection optional to the home owner. Should he become incapacitated by illness or accident, his mortgage loan will be paid regularly for a specified period.

Since insurance companies charge different rates for almost the same coverage, it is worthwhile to compare premium rates before choosing an underwriter. Some firms issue rebates in dividends at the expiration date of each policy. Refunds are then applied to reduce the renewal premium. Policies are generally for three-year terms, five years in states where allowed. A premium may be paid in full when due or on a deferred payment plan, usually annual payments which are slightly higher.

Not every insurance company covers the same risks, and some policies afford more protection than others. Adequate protection is not necessarily gained from the least expensive policy. Only certain risks are covered in a basic policy, so it becomes necessary to buy additional coverage. Comparison shopping will enable you to buy the best coverage at least cost.

Be sure that the insurance agent itemizes risks *not* covered by his company's policy. Additional coverage is available for loss or damage due to freezing or leakage of plumbing and heating systems; rain through windows, doors, or leaking roof; damage to any part of the structure from weight of ice, snow, or sleet; damage by falling objects such as trees; collapse of the house itself; loss of trees and shrubs and damage to landscaping; and other hazards.

Insurance for these risks is obtained by special endorsement, with each risk specifically written into the policy to be valid. Uninsurable risks are damages caused by floods, seepage into basements from water below the ground, and water back-up from sewers.

HEAT AND UTILITIES

The costs of heat and utilities are in addition to the mortgage payment and are paid directly by the home owner. The amount of fuel used depends upon the size of the house, insulation, and the climate. Utility bills for electricity, gas, and water will vary according to use. These are familiar problems to a mortgage lender, who can estimate their probable amount. New home owners who have left the city for the suburbs should provide for higher telephone bills in their household budget.

COMMUTING COSTS

How much you spend for commutation depends on the distance you travel from your home to your place of employment; and whether you use public transportation, your car, or join a car pool. Commutation costs should be estimated as soon as you choose the location of your home. In assessing commutation expenses, take into account your present fare.

MAINTENANCE

A house, like everything else, wears with age. Keeping it in good condition is a matter of planned maintenance and timely repairs.

Clapboard houses need painting every few years and worn, ripped, or broken roof shingles must be replaced. The heating, plumbing, and electrical systems demand periodic attention. Household appliances will need repairs or replacement.

In new, well-constructed houses these expenses usually are minimal during the first few years but increase as the structure becomes older. Nonetheless, a sum should be set aside each month to cope with unexpected problems. Construction experts estimate the average annual expenses are rarely higher than 2 percent of the home's total cost.

Chapter 19

Taxes

REAL ESTATE TAXES

All local governments are empowered to tax real property within their borders. These taxes are set by local assessors who place valuations on houses and land. Assessed valuation varies in different localities. Older homes may be assessed at a low 25 percent of their actual value, and new structures at a much higher percentage. The assessor's figure is based on what he believes is the true cash value of the property at the time he assessed it.

Growing communities with young couples and small children have the highest tax rates. As the population multiplies so will the need for such public services as schools, hospitals, sewage systems, fire and police protection. Taxes are relatively stable in older communities where these facilities are already established.

An assessment differs from a tax in that the home owner pays, in addition to his regular taxes, a sum for a specific local improvement that will benefit an immediate area. Special assessments are imposed for street lights, paving sidewalks, and installing curbs and sewers. These are payments for local benefits that increase property value. The assessment cost is treated as a *capital outlay* by the Internal Revenue Service and not as an expense like taxes. Therefore, the assessment is not a deductible expense for annual federal income tax purposes, as are real estate taxes.

Should you buy a dwelling where sewers are scheduled to replace cesspools, a special assessment will be imposed on your property. If sewers are already installed and a search of the public record reveals that no assessment has been paid by the seller, he is obligated to pay this assessment before the closing. Taxes and assessments levied during the seller's ownership should be paid by him, not the buyer.

TAX EXEMPTIONS

One of the boons to disabled veterans is the generous tax exemption given them by more than half the states. Many states grant limited exemptions to all veterans. Home-owning veterans in New York State enjoy one of the highest exemptions—up to $5,000. Despite the tax rate and special assessments, exemptions amount to substantial savings through the years.

An exemption is available to many veterans of World War I, World War II, the Korean and the Vietnam conflicts. Veterans' widows and their minor children are also eligible to share these tax benefits. Many veterans or their survivors are unaware of these benefits. Veterans can learn whether they are eligible for an exemption by contacting the nearest Veterans Administration office.

Recently, senior citizens have been granted special tax exemptions on their homes by some communities.

TAX DEDUCTIONS

As a home owner you may deduct from your income tax all real estate taxes and interest paid on every loan. Other deductible losses include damage to your property caused by hurricane, tornado, flood, lightning, earthquake, sonic boom, accident, burglary, termite destruction, and similar casualties. Losses not deductible are normal wear and tear on your house and loss of trees and shrubbery from disease or insects.

As soon as you become a home owner, you should take photographs of your property from all angles. These pictures will support your claim for tax deductions in the event of damage. Photographs showing your home after repairs or restoration will be additional evidence in your behalf.

In an inflationary period, most houses are resold at a price higher than that paid. The profit made on the sale of real property is considered income for federal tax purposes. But if the property is owned six months or longer before the sale, the profit is treated as a *capital gain* by the Internal Revenue Service and is taxed at the lower capital gains rate.

If you buy another used house within a two-year period beginning one year before and one year after the sale, your profit is not taxed at the time of the sale if you paid the same price or more. You will be permitted a longer period if (1) you build a new house or (2) if you enter the United States Armed Forces after you sell your home. You also gain more during inflationary times, since you are allowed to postpone payment on any profit from real estate until you sell your last home.

For example, a house bought in 1948 for $12,000 was sold for $22,000 in 1967. Within a year the seller bought another home for $22,000. His $10,000 profit was not treated as a gain for income tax purposes. Had the new dwelling cost only $18,000, the seller's profit of $4,000 would be subject to a maximum capital gain tax of 25 percent. If the seller had sold his home at a loss instead of a gain, he would not have been permitted to deduct the loss from his taxable income.

Chapter 20

Financing Home Improvements

Cash is the most economical way to pay for home improvements, though this is an impossible ambition for many people. Emergencies, such as a worn-out boiler or leaking roof, require immediate replacement and repair. Among the various loans available, one of the least expensive is the Federal Housing Administration (FHA) Title I Loan, which contains no hidden closing costs, charges, or other extras.

FHA TITLE I LOANS

Class 1 (a) Loans

More than 28 million FHA loans have been used to improve one-family homes. If the planned improvement costs $5,000 or less, a FHA Title I loan is available from banks and other qualified lending agencies. No down payment is required, and only the lender's approval is necessary on most loans. Usually the borrower's signature serves as security; no co-signers are needed, and the mortgage or deed of trust on the home is not disturbed.

To obtain a FHA Title I loan, the borrower must own his home or have a long lease which will run six months beyond the term of the loan, enjoy a good credit rating, and earn enough to repay the loan in the time period specified. Application for the loan is made with the lender who submits the forms to FHA for approval, if necessary. FHA forms, as well as help in preparing them, are obtained from a contractor, a dealer, or the lender.

Loans range from $100 to $5,000 for a maximum term of 84 months. The lender is permitted to charge a discount of $5.50 per $100 for each year on the first $2,500 of the loan, and $4.50 per $100 on the sum above $2,500. A discount means the interest amount is deducted in advance. Thus the borrower will receive only $94.50 but must repay $100. This interest rate amounts to approximately 11 percent for the first $2,500 and 9 percent for the remainder.

Protective features give the borrower advantages not always available in other lending plans. Contractors on the FHA blacklist will not be permitted to arrange loans or be approved for payment. But no home owner can be protected against himself. Since he will purchase the materials from dealers and hire the workmen himself or hire a contractor, he must also judge for himself whether materials and workmanship are satisfactory.

One of the most effective means to assure satisfactory work is the completion certificate. No payment will be made to a contractor unless he presents this certificate to the lender, signed by the home owner, declaring his work satisfactory.

Title I loans "must protect or improve the property's livability or utility," which excludes luxuries such as a swimming pool. Nor will a loan be given for work already done. If the work has been completed, the application will be rejected.

Title I loans may be used to buy built-in wall ovens, dishwashers, refrigerators, and similar items or to finance electrical work, roofing, and major landscape or site improvements. To ascertain whether or not your planned improvement can be financed with a Title I loan, consult the FHA or your lender.

The note you sign for the lender will show the due date for the first monthly payment, usually within two months from the date of the note. Repayment of the loan before the due date will result in a rebate from the lender, computed from tables approved by FHA.

FHA 203 (k) LOANS

The FHA 203 (k) loan, generally used for major home improvements over $5,000, was initiated in 1961 to rehabilitate houses ten or more years old. Newer homes will be considered if the loan is for "major structural improvements, correction of defects not known at the time of construction, or repair of damage caused by fire, flood, windstorm, or other casualty."

Loans range from $1,000 to $10,000 and are payable in monthly installments from 3 to 20 years. Application for this type of loan can be made at any FHA-approved bank or lending institution. However, the FHA 203 (k) loan is not popular with lending agencies because it is equivalent to a second mortgage at magnanimously reduced rates, which is a boon to the borrower.

A FHA 203 (k) loan must be FHA-approved and is secured by a lien. The interest rate is a straight 9 percent (8½ percent plus ½ percent for insurance), and the loan cannot be discounted. Closing costs are normally less than those for refinancing.

Under a 203 (k) loan, work must be done according to approved FHA specifications and usually under FHA inspection. Work already started is not eligible.

FHA 203 (b) LOANS

FHA loans for refinancing mortgages are available under 203 (b) for terms of three to thirty years.

Factors to be considered before applying for a refinancing loan are: the amount of existing debt; whether the existing loan is a VA, FHA, or conventional loan; whether the loan can be prepaid and, if so, what prepayment premium is required. The closing costs for this type of loan are less than those for a new home purchase. Overall financing costs, however, are greater than for 203 (k) loans, and the loan can be discounted by the lender.

Moreover, work already started may be financed with a 203 (b) loan, as well as luxury or unessential items. These improvements must add to the value of the property but not necessarily add to its livability and usefulness.

CONVENTIONAL LOANS

Savings and commercial banks widely advertise their home improvement loans. These are intended for the home owner with a regular income and a good credit record. In doubtful cases, the lender may require a co-signer, as would the FHA. All loans are secured by the borrower's house.

The maximum amount of the loan is about $5,000 at interest rates higher than those of FHA and depending on the terms. Discounted in advance, the actual interest rate is doubled. A number of banks include life insurance in their loans to assure repayment in case the borrower becomes incapacitated.

OPEN-END MORTGAGE LOANS

An open-end mortgage loan permits the home owner to borrow money at a future date, usually up to the amount paid on the principal. The borrower can finance improvements by using his existing mortgage. Interest rates are usually the same as that of the original loan. Although the term expires on the same date as the original mortgage, the loan can be extended. Your equity in your home is the security.

Chapter 21

Endangered Ownership

LIENS

Unlike stocks, bank accounts, and other chattels, a house is a
stationary asset against which creditors can proceed for payment
of legal debts. One of the direst threats to a home owner is a lien
or legal claim that renders his home unmarketable. In certain cases
the lien empowers a creditor to sell the debtor's house. Unsuspecting
home owners sometimes are duped into signing agreements with
unscrupulous contractors or grasping creditors giving a lien on their
house.

Another means by which a creditor obtains a lien on a house is a
judgment. A successful lawsuit against the debtor enables the creditor to file or docket the judgment, imposing a lien on any real estate
owned by the debtor. If the debt is large enough, it becomes possible
for the creditor to have a marshal or sheriff sell the property to satisfy
the judgment.

Legal difficulties of this sort never strike suddenly. They ensue
usually after an unpleasant dispute with a contractor or other
creditor. You can avoid this plight by never signing any contract
unless you fully understand it. If an agreement, such as a second
mortgage or a lien, even hints that you are to surrender an interest
in your property, do not sign it without consulting your lawyer. If

you are served with a summons or any other legal process, whether
you believe it to be real or false, show it to your lawyer. People
who pay their debts, even belatedly, almost never find themselves
in this impasse.

Taxes and assessments are imposed on real property by state and
local governments to defray costs of operation. Unpaid taxes become
a lien on your property. A buyer of property bearing a tax lien should
notify the seller to pay the tax before the closing, otherwise the new
owner becomes liable for the unpaid debt. Failure to pay Federal
income taxes, estate or gift taxes, empowers the government to place
a lien on your house for the taxes due, plus interest and penalties. Tax
liens take precedence over all others.

Mechanic's Lien

Any person who furnishes materials or labor to repair and improve
real property is entitled to a lien on the house if he has not been paid.
Mechanics' liens were created by law to protect the workman who
performed services on real property. Although an unpaid contractor
has the right to directly sue the non-paying owner, the law grants him
a lien to forestall the possibility that the owner may sell his house
and decamp, leaving his creditors powerless to collect. The new owner
is not liable for his predecessor's debts.

But if the house is sold with a lien on it, which is unlikely, the new
owner is liable for the debt. For this reason, title companies require
the seller to show receipted bills for repairs or improvements made at
least six months prior to the sale. If these are not available, the company may withhold enough money at the time of settlement to pay
creditors. A lien can be placed only on the improved property. It
cannot be applied to any other parcel of property belonging to the
same owner.

CONDEMNATION

No property is safe from condemnation. Condemnation is the
procedure by which land needed for public use may be taken, with
or without the owner's permission, by federal, state, and local govern-

ments or their agencies. Under the law of eminent domain, a shadowy risk hovers over properties that are located where areas are changing, creating the need for highways, bridge approaches, wider streets, urban redevelopment, airports, sewage disposal plants, sewers, schools, and other public uses.

Often a startled home owner learns for the first time that his property will be condemned when the appraiser rings his doorbell to place a value on his house. Pictures are taken and sketches are made. In time the owner is visited by negotiators to offer a price set by the appraisers. If he agrees, title is quickly transferred.

A refusal to sell results in condemnation proceedings, legally depriving the owner of his property. He may take court action, but only to claim a higher price. Since eminent domain is a drastic governmental power, no court will support a home owner who declines to sell. However, your property may not be taken by any governmental agency, even if you are offered more than your house is worth, unless the acquisition is for public use. Only that part of your property needed for public use may be taken.

Your home cannot be legally taken to be sold to any person for his private use. But you can lose your property if it is needed for airports, railroads, and other projects that are owned by private companies but used for public benefit. Should an electric or telephone company desire to erect a cable pole on your property they may take only an easement, the right of way over, on, or under your land to maintain their cables.

Owners are not always offered fair prices in condemnation proceedings. How much you will get for your property depends largely on the appraiser. If your home and land are taken, you are entitled to full compensation for the market value. Broad differences of opinion may exist among appraisers regarding the same property.

Condemnation laws vary in different states but a home owner who is dissatisfied with the appraiser's estimate has legal means to argue his position. When private negotiations fail with a state agency, you can always resort to court action. Each state's condemnation laws decree the kind of hearing to be held to settle the case. In some, the deciding body may be a jury; in others a judge, or a panel of commissioners. If you object to any ruling, you may appeal the decision to a higher court.

EASEMENT

An easement is the right to use land belonging to someone else. A common example is a utility or telephone company having an easement to erect poles and string power lines over your property. Easements have often been granted by local governments or by a former owner of the land to a public utility company.

When only part of your land is taken for a telephone, power, or rail line, the problem can become a bewildering entanglement. Besides payment for the amount of land taken, you are entitled to damages for the decreased value of the rest of your land. Fair compensation, according to many appraisers, involves determining the market value of the entire parcel of land, then paying proportionately for the amount taken, plus compensatory damage for what is left. Nonetheless, however generously an owner is paid, he will derive no comfort from a railroad track laid across his garden.

Easements are recorded in the county clerk's office, and are usually disclosed in the title search when you apply for a mortgage loan. Some title companies, however, merely note: "Subject to covenants, restrictions and agreements of record, if any." If this phrase appears in the seller's deed or the title search, request a copy of all records.

Easement by Prescription

An easement by prescription is acquired by right of long use. A person who uses another's property for the benefit of his own land for a given number of years, acquires an easement by prescription. Sometimes this easement may not be recorded until it becomes a dispute, finally ending in a costly lawsuit. Such an easement occurs when a home owner allows another person, perhaps a neighbor, to use his land for a specific purpose.

Length of time is an important factor in establishing the legality of such a right. Possessive use by the non-owner must continue uninterruptedly for a period of time according to each state's law. Most states set this time between ten and twenty years. If an owner does not act to prohibit such use of his land within the state's statutory period, the easement becomes an incontestable claim by the non-owner to use the land for an explicit purpose.

This type of easement may result when a driveway is shared by a neighbor, or a right-of-way is continuously used through property. A neighbor may build a driveway which is partly on your property. If he uses it for the prescribed number of years, he may have an easement that you cannot legally terminate.

FORECLOSURE

Foreclosure is an ominous word. It means loss of a home enforced by law when a borrower has failed to meet his mortgage payments. Such a personal disaster may seem remote to a home owner earning a steady income and careful in his expenditures. But many families for divers reasons have suffered the blow of foreclosure. During the thirty-year period from 1929 to 1959, more than 2½ million families lost their dwellings in this manner.

Many foreclosures could be avoided if the owner understood the causes leading to this debacle. Unexpected financial reverses, such as loss of employment, business failure, or a nationwide crisis, may strike anyone, although it is highly doubtful whether the catastrophic depression of 1929 could recur. Many financial cushions now exist that were unknown in 1929.

Grave sickness or death often deprives a family of its breadwinner. But this need not result in foreclosure because insurance is now available to home owners. In case of death, the mortgage will be paid in full by the insurance company.

Marital discord is the largest single cause of mortgage default. Not surprisingly, the family's economic stability is upset by separation or divorce. Few wives, left alone to assume all responsibilities of managing a home, are capable of dealing with these problems, particularly if there are small children who require constant care.

Some home owners cannot manage their money matters. Budget is a word alien to these people who often live beyond their means. They spend money without pause or thought, swirling downward so deeply that "they have to reach up to touch bottom." Lending institutions never give such persons a second chance to default.

Borrowing more money than can be repaid is another cause of foreclosure. Although lending agencies usually deny loans in amounts beyond the applicant's capacity to pay, some lenders succumb to the temptation because the borrower has a steady income, ignoring the stark fact that he is actually over-borrowing.

No lending institution relishes a foreclosure. Most will bend over backwards to help the harried borrower. Alternate arrangements are proposed as mortgage payments fall due, provided the borrower's credit status, the value of his home, and other factors meet minimum requirements. These measures are: (1) Interest payments, but postponement of principal until a later, convenient date. (2) Refinancing the loan. If warranted by the dwelling's market value, the remaining loan may be refinanced. The installments will be extended over a greater length, reducing the monthly payments to an amount the home owner can conveniently afford.

Selling Your Home

Chapter 22

When You Sell Your Home

WHY HOUSES ARE SOLD

The accelerated trend of family mobility in recent years has led to an increasing change in home ownership. Many families no longer plan to live in the same dwelling all their lives. Although different reasons motivate a family in selling its home, there are important and influencing factors that determine whether the seller receives a high or low price.

Every buyer wants to know why the owner is selling. Among the more common reasons is a new job or a promotion requiring the owner to leave the area or state. Often a retired couple will dispose of a large domicile for a smaller home in Florida or similar balmy region. Such explanations are satisfactory to prospective buyers, who may have a lurking suspicion of a distress sale due to serious structural defects or a changing neighborhood.

Improved financial conditions are another reason for selling. When income rises, the family usually seeks a more expensive dwelling. However, if this is your reason for selling, a buyer may evince resentment because many people don't want a house considered inferior by its former owner. If decreased income forces a sale for a more modest home, a wise seller does not mention this fact either. A buyer may infer that the house is too expensive to maintain.

213

A spacious house bought by a large family often becomes burdensome and lonely as the children mature and leave for college or marriage. At such times a couple offers their house for sale, planning to move to a smaller house. Unless this reason is tactfully explained, a buyer may conclude the house is too large or too expensive to manage, especially if he himself has a small family.

There are few factors that adversely affect a dwelling's value more than a changing neighborhood. Since the selling price tends to seek the level of most of the other neighborhood structures, a house that cost $40,000 to build will not bring its full value if located among $20,000 homes. More often, a less expensive house commands a higher price if surrounded by more costly dwellings.

A home owner disposing of his property because lower-priced homes are being built in the immediate area will more likely receive full value if he sells early. Prospective buyers rarely perceive depreciating trends at the beginning.

Changes from residential to commercial areas are another cause for depreciating values. This shift usually occurs at a community's fringes. In most cases, the builders have obtained variances (modifications of zoning ordinances or building codes) to construct gas stations, repair shops, and other commercial structures. In time a new street may be constructed, leading to rezoning of both sides to permit retail shops. As commercial enterprises are attracted to the area, families dispose of their property to move elsewhere. Only those home owners who sell their property before the trend becomes noticeable are likely to recoup their complete investment.

SELLING POINTS

The Season

Time and patience are a distinct advantage to a seller. A home owner who must sell quickly or is impatient will rarely regain his full investment. (An exception is a house in a highly desirable area where demand exceeds supply.) Generally no real estate market exists, in the manner of the stock exchange, ready to buy a house the moment it is offered.

Spring is usually the best time to sell a house. Pleasantly warm weather inevitably draws people into the open, many intent on buying. Families with children develop a strong impulse for home ownership. People prefer to settle in their new dwelling before the fall school term begins. The second best period is autumn. Families who buy want to move in before the cold weather descends.

During summer most families concern themselves with vacations and other hot-weather activities. In winter people are understandably hesitant to look for a home. Houses are sold in all seasons, but you have the best chance of selling in the spring.

Appearance

The old adage, "Never judge a book by its cover," does not apply to a house for sale. First impressions cause many a potential buyer to walk away without entering the premises. An unkempt, dilapidated appearance will block a sale unless the house is offered as a "handyman's special" at a bargain price. A first impression will be favorable if the exterior is cleanly painted, broken shingles are replaced, sagging roof gutters are refastened, the shrubbery and lawn are trimmed, and other unsightly conditions are corrected.

Dimly lighted interiors, cluttered kitchens redolent with the mixed odors of recently cooked foods, dripping faucets, and children's toys strewn about the floors may repel prospective buyers. Keep the household air fresh and clean-smelling and do not cook foods that have over-powering odors. Also try to avoid strong-smelling disinfectants and medicines because many people associate these odors with sickness.

Tidy attics, closets, and basements create good impressions, allowing the prospective buyer to estimate their size. Disarrayed litter in these areas immediately suggests that the house lacks adequate storage space. Implicit in a woman buyer's mind is the fear that the dwelling may be infested with vermin or rodents. Such concern will vanish in an immaculate home.

A noisy domicile scarcely conveys an impression of restfulness and serenity. Avoid such distracting and unnecessary noises as the TV, radio, hi-fi sets, clamorous children, bawling infants, and barking dogs. Stairways which are free of objects and well-lighted reduce the danger of a lost sale because the prospect tripped.

When showing the house during the day, allow maximum sunlight to enter. At night use outdoor lights and a well-lighted interior to convey a sense of cheer and warmth. In hot weather turn on the attic and room fans or air-conditioners. During winter keep the interior temperature no higher than 70°, mindful that your prospects are wearing heavy outer clothing.

Unless there are urgent reasons, avoid the unnecessary expense of painting the interior. Color preferences are often intensely personal and may drive away the prospective buyer. Many sales have evaporated because the buyer's wife wanted to redecorate before moving in, but her husband vetoed an expenditure since the interior was freshly painted. Only neutral colors, such as whites, grays, and beiges, should be used if redecorating is necessary.

A furnished house sells much more quickly than an empty one. Comfortably furnished, the interior suffuses a warm, secure impression. An unfurnished house may suggest that the owner was driven to leave for unfavorable reasons and is desperately anxious to sell. Almost invariably, offers in such a case are much lower than would be made for a reassuringly furnished home.

Remodeling Possibilities

Very often a home buyer will consider an older house, intending to remodel it for his family's requirements. In some dwellings the addition of a bedroom, bath, or recreation room is relatively inexpensive. A ranch house with an unfinished attic lends itself to such remodeling. But the structural rearrangement of other houses may cost large sums. Besides, many local zoning ordinances ban such remodeling. If your home lends itself to remodeling possibilities, consider this advantage in setting your selling price. A hesitant buyer, after seeing an unfinished expansion attic, may decide the house is adequate for his family's needs.

Chapter 23

Financial Factors in Selling Your Home

SELLING PRICE

Determining the selling price of your home is often a frustrating decision. Neither art nor science characterize real estate transactions. The entire purpose is to receive the highest possible price. Several factors offer a rough guideline to decide the market value of property. Prices of older homes tend to reflect their present cost of replacement. If a twenty-year-old house, which cost $15,000 when new, can be constructed today for $20,000, it could not readily sell for $30,000. But a well-maintained home built in the late 1930s now sells up to three or more times its original price—equal to its cost of construction today.

The selling price of one or more comparable houses in the immediate area is a fairly accurate index of your property's market value. Federal tax stamps, affixed to a deed when ownership is transferred, show the price of a previous sale. The stamps cost $1.10 for every $1,000. If a deed has $22.00 worth of stamps, the owner paid $20,000. Simply divide $22.00 by $1.10. Deeds are public documents that can be examined at the office of the County Clerk or County Registrar of Deeds.

Although this Federal tax was repealed at the end of 1967, many states have re-imposed it. Some states, such as New Jersey, now require the full price of the property to be listed on the deed.

Purchasing extra tax stamps to deceive prospective buyers is common practice in transactions involving apartment houses and commercial and industrial buildings. Stamps, hundreds or thousands of dollars above the required amount, are purchased and affixed to deeds. But most home owners are not speculators, and few resort to this practice.

If the property has been sold subject to an existing mortgage, some deeds will show the mortgage amount. Knowing the sale price of nearby homes will help you get the highest possible price for yours.

You can further strengthen your position by obtaining from the FHA, before you list the house for sale, a statement of the mortgage amount which this government agency will insure for an acceptable buyer. In an inflationary market with rising mortgage costs, an FHA-insured loan at lower interest rates will attract many prospects.

REAL ESTATE BROKERS

Arrangements with real estate brokers can be favorable to you or not, depending upon the kind of agreement you enter. An established real estate agent is in a good position to appraise local property value. He usually is better informed about comparable sales and price trends. By helping you set a reasonable price on your home at the beginning, he will facilitate its sale.

Seeking a buyer for your dwelling is the broker's main purpose. A conscientious agent will advertise your property and screen "lookers" who are not serious buyers. Negotiating the selling price is another function of the broker. Many sellers are temperamentally unsuited to haggle. Acting as a middleman, the broker will often effect a compromise acceptable to both parties.

The disadvantages of dealing through a broker begin with cost. If he sells your property, his fee is between 5 percent and 6 percent of the price, the percentage varies in different states. Thus if the sale price is $30,000, his commission will be $1,500 or $1,800. In many cases, the brokers' untiring efforts fully merit their commission. Among the different types of brokerage agreements are:

1. *Multiple Listing.* This arrangement among real estate agents in a community allows each broker to offer his listings to all other members. If a sale results, the commission is divided between the broker who entered the listing and the one who sold the house. Such a listing widens your market, but you chance involvement with brokers whom you would not voluntarily choose to represent you.

2. *Open Listing.* This method is the most advantageous arrangement for the seller, who lists his property with any number of brokers with the understanding that only the one who brings about the sale will receive a commission. Open listings have no time limit and may be terminated at will. If you use the open listing, do not cancel the agreement so that you can sell your dwelling to the buyer without paying a commission to the broker who brought him to you; the broker is legally entitled to a commission.

3. *Net Listing.* This type of listing refers to a price below which an owner will not sell his house and at which price a broker will not be paid a commission. The agent receives a sum over and above the net listing. Thus a seller notifies the broker that he wants $30,000 for his house. The broker must add his commission to this price. If he sells the dwelling at the buyer's stated price, the broker is not entitled to any commission. A seller may combine this type of listing with an open listing.

4. *Exclusive Agency.* This is an agreement with a broker whom you employ exclusively as the only one authorized to sell your property for a specified period. You agree not to retain any other agent during the time the agreement is in force. If you sell your house, no commission is payable to him. But if another broker finds a buyer during this term of employment, the agent of the agreement is entitled to a full commission besides the commission due the broker who sold the property. In return for this exclusive agency the broker agrees to work diligently to find a buyer. Some brokers will use their best efforts, others will not.

5. *Exclusive Right to Sell.* This agreement is similar to the exclusive agency, except for one important provision: if you sell your property during the term of the broker's employment, he is entitled to a full commission although he did nothing to find a buyer. This type of agreement is frequently sought by brokers, but should be avoided by the seller.

6. *Commission Dependent on Transfer of Title.* Although a

broker's commission is payable when he finds a buyer who agrees to your terms, a number of causes may intervene to prevent the sale. If this happens you may lose a substantial sum without selling your home, unless you are protected by a special agreement which stipulates that the broker's commission is payable only if and when the title closes. Nevertheless, the broker is entitled to his full commission if the owner willfully refuses to sell his house after the contract is signed.

THE GUARANTEED TRADE-IN

In recent years some builders and brokers have devised trade-in arrangements so that a home owner can trade in one dwelling for another. This system evolved from the automobile trade-in which is familiar to most people. But trading in a house for another is much more complex than trading in an auto.

Because the trade-in plan has become popular, the National Institute of Real Estate Brokers has formed the International Traders Club, with "Trading Posts" in many states. Among the three plans which they offer, only the guaranteed trade-in should be considered. Under this plan, the broker guarantees to buy your house directly at an agreed price unless he sells it within a specified period, usually sixty or ninety days. You, in turn, must agree to buy the home he offers.

You will be required to sign an exclusive agency agreement to assure him of a commission resulting from the sale of your property. When you select a home from the properties on his listing, the broker will guarantee to sell your dwelling for a sum that is about 10 percent lower than the current market price. Studies of trade-in plans, however, reveal the home owner's costs actually range from 15 percent to 20 percent of the selling price. This includes the 5 or 6 percent selling commission, and payment for assorted repairs and improvements incurred by the broker to facilitate the sale. To assure that the sale is properly timed, you must sell and buy directly from the broker, and this makes the transaction costly.

An owner with an FHA-insured mortgage can trade in his house without paying off the insured mortgage. The FHA and the lender, who holds the mortgage, can agree to substitute the new owner's name on the mortgage. The seller is then released from all personal liability on the mortgage.

Although you have committed yourself to buy another home, don't succumb to the blandishments of the broker or builder by buying a new house before agreeing on the price of the one you are selling. A hoary but effective selling scheme is to concentrate glibly on the new home's attractiveness, not allowing the buyer an opportunity to consider the price critically.

In the manner of nimble-tongued salesmen who studiously avoid trade-in price until the customer is persuaded he wants the new car, some real estate brokers will "sell" you the new house before turning their attention to dickering on the price of the one you are selling. Insist upon setting the price of your present dwelling before discussing the cost of the new one.

Allowing yourself to be diverted can be costly. If, for example, your present dwelling is worth $30,000 the trade-in may cost you an additional $2,550 besides the broker's commission of $1,500 or $1,800. Trading or exchanging your property could be a dismaying experience. Not infrequently, a broker may change from your agent to your adversary. All of these possibilities stress once again the need for a competent lawyer to guide you through every stage in this kind of transaction.

Property secured by a VA loan should not be sold unless the mortgage is paid in full or the VA releases the seller in writing from future responsibility on the loan. If the seller's loan is not paid in full and he has no release in writing, he is liable for all payments to the government if the buyer or any subsequent owner defaults. It makes no difference that the buyer assumed personal liability for repayment of the VA loan.

If you plan to sell your home with a VA mortgage, write to the VA office that guaranteed your loan. Don't sign a contract of sale until you are released in writing from personal liability by the VA.

SELLING THE HOUSE YOURSELF

Many home owners successfully sell their homes themselves and save the 5 or 6 percent commission. This arrangement should be attempted only if you have sufficient time to devote to it. Advertisements in local newspapers should list the most attractive qualities of your home. Since most prospective buyers read the Friday, Saturday, and Sunday editions, time your insertions for the weekend to get maximum results.

Other opportunities are available for free advertising. Many houses are sold by word of mouth. Local community organizations, churches, and lodges usually have bulletin boards for assorted ads. National corporations continually transfer personnel; they welcome listings of one-family homes which newcomers may see. Many supermarkets allow house listings to be posted on their community bulletin boards.

Placing a "For Sale" sign on the lawn often draws buyers. If you plan to use a sign, have it made by a professional sign painter or buy it at a hardware store, as it will contribute to the attractive, clean-cut appearance of your property. To many, a crudely lettered sign reflects the character of the property it advertises. This form of advertising is banned in some communities, so be sure its use is permitted before having a sign made.

Why do people choose or reject a house? Well, the building industry, which was especially eager to know, retained experts in marketing and psychology to ferret out buyers' motivations. In-depth interviews were conducted to learn what features people consider important in a house; which sales appeal will evoke the desired response compared to the fears that deter a couple from buying. Shown in Table 11 are the results, listing selling points to be stressed and subjects to be avoided because they arouse negative reactions.

TABLE 11

MARKETING IDEAS FROM
THE "PROJECT HOME" STUDY

MARKET	WHAT TO EMPHASIZE	WHAT TO DE-EMPHASIZE
Bride/ Newly-wed	Privacy New forms of housing units to help instill good housing habits Family help on financing Mobile homes Interiors Independence	Duty Planned activities "Roots" and "security" Care and maintenance Resale later on The words "retirement" and "youth"
First House	Children (sleeping rooms, play space, recreational facilities) Location Reassurance on financing Appliances and built-ins	Costs (many prospects fear ability to pay) References to youthfulness of buyer Be prepared to combat predilection toward older houses
Up-Grade	Ease of moving (because men resist moving) Games or contests to stimulate new-house interest Bring model to prospect (as in a shopping center, for example) Call on men at their offices Help in disposing of present house	Togetherness The house as the woman's domain (yet retain subtle appeal to the woman, who is the one who usually most wants to move)
Retiree	A house is a wise way to use available funds Convenience to city Climate Glamourize low-cost housing	A truly rural environment Maintenance and costs Dependence on others Moving

MARKET	WHAT TO EMPHASIZE	WHAT TO DE-EMPHASIZE
Two-family house	Financial facts, income potential Stability of neighborhood Free or at-cost maintenance where such is offered The word "house" has more meaning than "home"	Bother of tenants Finding and pleasing renters Financial commitment, which buyers are apt to fear
Vacation home	Year-round use New forms of mobile homes or prefabs where applicable Modern design Masculine appeal (and use of appropriate promotional methods)	Household chores Upkeep costs Use of home for eventual retirement use

Source—American Builder

Home Buyer's Checklist

No home is perfect, but this checklist of major items will help you select the best possible dwelling. If the score sheet shows too many defects, you will be amply forewarned before you make a final decision.

	Plus	Minus
1. Location		
Is the area subject to high tides, floods, mudslides?	_____	_____
Does the area have adequate water supplies?	_____	_____
Are any major public projects, such as highways, reservoirs, airports, etc., proposed for the area in the near future?	_____	_____
2. Community		
Is the community changing or deteriorating?	_____	_____
Is the local government having fiscal difficulties?	_____	_____
Does the community have sufficient tax ratables (business and industry) to help with the tax burden?	_____	_____
Are land values increasing?	_____	_____
What are the tax rates?	_____	_____
Does the community have the cultural, educational, and medical facilities *you* consider essential?	_____	_____
Does the community have a good school system?	_____	_____
Does the community have active civic groups?	_____	_____
Are the residents proud of their community?	_____	_____

3. Neighborhood
   Is the neighborhood changing or deteriorating?   _____   _____
   Does it have a pleasing atmosphere?   _____   _____
   Are there any recreational facilities nearby?   _____   _____
   Is the property low-lying, subject to flood?   _____   _____
   Are there disturbing noises, smoke, or noxious
      fumes in the area?   _____   _____
   Are railroads, airports, and heavy traffic nearby?   _____   _____
   Are the adjoining homes well-maintained?   _____   _____
   Will much through traffic endanger children?   _____   _____
   Is a safe play area available for the children?   _____   _____
4. Accessibility
   Is public transportation in the area adequate?   _____   _____
   Are parking facilities at train and bus terminals
      adequate?   _____   _____
   Are interconnecting highways readily accessible?   _____   _____
   What are the traffic conditions?   _____   _____
   Are transportation costs reasonable?   _____   _____
   Is public transportation convenient?   _____   _____
   Is shopping convenient?   _____   _____
   Is there an adequate variety of stores and personal
      service facilities?   _____   _____
   Are there schools nearby?   _____   _____
   Are houses of worship convenient?   _____   _____
5. Public and Utility Facilities
   Does the community have adequate police pro-
      tection?   _____   _____
   Does the community provide fire protection?   _____   _____
   If so, is it a paid department?   _____   _____
   Is the fire hydrant nearby?   _____   _____
   Is there a volunteer ambulance corps?   _____   _____
   Are medical facilities convenient?   _____   _____
   Are gas, electricity, and water lines in?   _____   _____
   Are utility rates reasonable?   _____   _____
   Is there a municipal sewer?   _____   _____
   Are sewers and drains adequate?   _____   _____
   Does the community provide garbage removal?   _____   _____
   Does it provide snow clearance?   _____   _____
   Are streets well-lighted after dark?   _____   _____
6. Restrictions
   Is the neighborhood protected by recorded land use
      covenants?   _____   _____
   Are there any violations of zoning laws or building
      codes filed against the property?   _____   _____
   Is the community zoned for residential use only?   _____   _____
   Are zoning laws enforced to protect the property?   _____   _____

Do restrictions apply to retail outlets and multiple dwellings? _____ _____

Are variances or modifications of zoning regulations easily granted? _____ _____

If adjoining area is zoned for commercial or industrial use are buffer zones (trees, shrubs, fences) required? _____ _____

7. Assessments and Other Costs

If utilities—water, gas, electricity, sewers—are installed, are they paid for? _____ _____

Are there any assessments or liens against the house? _____ _____

Are extra costs, such as landscaping or construction of walks and streets that were not yet installed when the sales contract was signed, included in the house price? _____ _____

Are the extra expenses clearly specified in the contract? _____ _____

8. House Appearance and Design

(Homes that vary too radically from adjoining dwellings frequently depreciate in value for lack of buyers. Those having the best resale value are similar in style to the surrounding houses.)

Does the architectural design of the house conform to that of others in the immediate area? _____ _____

If the house is different, does it blend with the surrounding designs? _____ _____

9. Exterior of House

Does the roof sag along its ridge? _____ _____

Are roof shingles in good condition? _____ _____

Are gutters and leaders (downspouts) firmly attached to structure and in good condition? _____ _____

Is the chimney erect? _____ _____

If there is a fireplace, are there two flues? _____ _____

Siding (Walls)

If siding is wood, is the paint in good condition? _____ _____

If it is stucco, does it need to be patched or replaced? _____ _____

If it is brick or masonry, are the mortar joints intact? _____ _____

If it is shingle, is the condition good? _____ _____

Windows and Doors

Do windows permit sufficient natural lighting and ventilation? _____ _____

Are the wooden windows free of decay? _____ _____

Do the windows move freely and close snugly? _____ _____

Do iron casement windows close tightly? _____ _____

Are the aluminum windows badly pitted? _____ _____

Are windows and doors fitted with weather stripping? _____ _____

Are there aluminum storm windows and screens? _____ _____

Drainage and Sewage

Does the ground slope gently away from the house? _____ _____

Does the rainwater run into dry wells or concrete splash pans? _____ _____

If there is a septic tank or cesspool, is it ample for your needs? _____ _____

Garage

Is the garage large enough for your car? _____ _____

Is the driveway sufficiently wide to maneuver freely? _____ _____

Does the driveway slope away from the garage? _____ _____

10. Interior of House

Are the attic floor and walls insulated? _____ _____

Is the attic free of condensation? _____ _____

Are water leakage marks visible, especially around the chimney? _____ _____

Is the heating system efficient? _____ _____

Is the hot water supply sufficient? _____ _____

Are water pipes of durable copper or brass? _____ _____

Is the electrical system adequate? _____ _____

Do all rooms have enough outlets? _____ _____

Are floors level and without serious flaws? _____ _____

Are the walls smoothly finished and free of cracks? _____ _____

Is there evidence of termite damage? _____ _____

Floor Plan

Is the overall layout, size and arrangement of rooms, closets, bathrooms, stairway and foyer, suitable? _____ _____

Is the dwelling large enough? _____ _____

Can extensions be added? _____ _____

Is the kitchen conveniently arranged and equipped? _____ _____

Is the dining area ample? _____ _____

Is laundry space adequate? _____ _____

Does each bedroom have at least one closet? _____ _____

Is the bathroom conveniently accessible? _____ _____

Is there a bathroom or half bathroom for each floor? _____ _____

Is a coat closet located in the entry hall? _____ _____

Is there at least one linen closet? _____ _____

Is storage space convenient and ample? _____ _____

Basement

Does the basement remain dry after heavy rains? _____ _____

Is the basement tight enough to prevent rodents and vermin from entering? _____ _____

Do steel columns support the main beam? _____ _____

Is the ceiling high enough so that the room can be altered to provide additional living space? _____ _____

Appendix II

Home Buyer's Financial Checklist

HOW MUCH CAN YOU AFFORD?

Compare these figures to your current assets, plus an estimate of your ability to pay in future years.

INITIAL COSTS:
    Down payment $_____
    Closing costs:
        Title search   _____
        Legal fees   _____
        Other expenses   _____
              TOTAL INITIAL COSTS $_____
MONTHLY COSTS:
    Amortization of Mortgage:
        Principal $_____
        Interest   _____
            TOTAL MORTGAGE PAYMENTS $_____
    Escrow account payments:
        Taxes $_____
        Assessments   _____
        Fire insurance   _____
        Other   _____
          TOTAL ESCROW PAYMENTS $_____
    TOTAL PAYMENTS TO LENDER $_____

229

OTHER EXPENSES:
    Estimated fuel costs (monthly average) $_____
    Utilities:
        Electricity $_____
        Fuel
        Water   _____
               TOTAL FOR UTILITIES $_____
    Liability insurance (monthly average) $_____
    Estimated maintenance and repairs (monthly average) $_____
    *Reserve for appliance replacement, apportioned
        monthly on life of appliance   _____
    Commutation costs   _____
               TOTAL MONTHLY COSTS $_____

* For example, if a major appliance cost $324 and has a useful life of 15 years, $21.60 a year, or $1.80 a month, should be placed in a reserve account where it will be available when the appliance needs replacement. Appliances to consider are washing machines, dryers, dishwashers, stoves, and refrigerators.

Is this entire monthly expenditure easily absorbed by your monthly income? Deduct the total monthly cost from your monthly take-home pay. Be certain that you have enough money left to meet all expenses in your family's budget.

Appendix III

Seller's Checklist

Use the Buyer's Checklist to evaluate the plus and minus factors of your property. Attractive surroundings and a tidy house increase sales appeal.

1. Exterior	Plus	Minus
Are the sidewalks in good repair?		
Are steps in good condition?		
Are windows and curtains clean?		
Are window shades evenly drawn?		
Are venetian blinds down and open?		
Is your doorbell in working order?		
Warm weather		
Are the lawns trimmed and edged?		
Are hedges clipped?		
Are straggly shrubs pruned?		
Are flower beds cultivated?		
Have faded flowers been removed?		
Are the grounds free of refuse?		
Are sidewalks swept?		
Are toys and tools put away?		
Cold Weather		
Are sidewalks free of snow and ice?		
Are entry areas free of snow and ice?		
Has winter sports equipment been put away?		
Garage		
Are tools, garden, and sports equipment neatly stored?		
Has the garage been swept?		

Have unnecessary accumulations been removed?   ____   ____
2. Interior
   Is the house free of cooking odors?   ____   ____
   Is it tidy?   ____   ____
   Are beds made?   ____   ____
   Have loose doorknobs, cabinet knobs, door and
      cabinet hinges been repaired?   ____   ____
   Are light switches in proper working order?   ____   ____
   Have dripping faucets been repaired?   ____   ____
   Are all stairways free of clutter?   ____   ____
   Are attic and basement tidy?   ____   ____
   Have you disposed of unnecessary accumulations?   ____   ____
   Are your storage and closet areas well displayed with
      items neatly arranged and unnecessary clutter
      removed?   ____   ____
   Are the bathrooms tidy?   ____   ____
   Are kitchen counters cleared?   ____   ____
   Is the kitchen ventilating fan free of grease and grime? ____   ____
   Are lights turned on in dark areas?   ____   ____
   Have burned out light bulbs been replaced?   ____   ____
3. General
   If the house is being inspected in the evening, is it
      well-illuminated inside and out?   ____   ____
   Are as few people as possible present during in-
      spections?   ____   ____
   Are the radio and television turned off?   ____   ____
   Are pets out of the way?   ____   ____

Glossary: Building Terms

acoustical materials: Sound-absorbing substances used to cover ceilings and walls.

aggregate: Ingredients of concrete; gravel and sand, mixed with portland cement.

air-dried lumber: Wood that is seasoned in open air instead of in a kiln.

anchor bolts: Bolts used to secure a wooden sill to a masonry foundation.

armored cable: Electrical wire protected by flexible galvanized steel, often called BX cable.

asbestos shingle: Fireproof roof or siding material made of portland cement and asbestos.

ashlar: Masonry of cut stone.

backfill: Excavated soil replaced in a trench or against the foundation.

balloon frame: A type of construction in which the studs rise in one piece from foundation to roof.

balusters: Upright supports or spindles of a stair railing; a banister.

balustrade: A row of balusters on which a rail rests.

baseboard: A molding at the bottom of a wall to present a finished appearance where wall and floor meet.

batt: Insulating material in blanket form, made in small sizes for convenient installation.

batten: A narrow strip of wood nailed across two other pieces to cover a joint or crack.

beam: Any substantial length of timber, steel, or other material which supports a load over an opening; a girder.

beamed ceiling: Exposed timber placed horizontally along a ceiling which may be load-bearing or merely decorative.

blanket: Flexible insulating material in rolls up to eighty feet in length, usually paper covered.

blue stain: Discoloration of wood by certain moldlike fungi which does not materially reduce the strength of the wood.

board foot: A unit of lumber measurement, one foot long, one foot wide, and one inch thick. Lumber in large quantities is sold by board feet.

breezeway: An open, roofed passageway.

brick veneer: A brick facing laid against exterior walls of a frame structure which is not designed to support any weight of the building. *See* solid brick.

bridging: Small strips of wood or metal fastened diagonally between joists to make them rigid; a method of bracing the floor. Wood is sometimes used as solid bridging.

British thermal unit (Btu): A method of measuring heat: the amount of heat needed to raise the temperature of one pound of water one degree Fahrenheit; the standard measurement to determine power of an air-conditioning unit.

building code: A set of rules and regulations established by local government, which determines the standards for procedures and materials in construction.

built-up roof: A flat or low pitched roof of three or more layers of tar-saturated felt or jute; the surface is finished with gravel or crushed slag.

cap: The top piece on a column, door cornice, molding, or lintel over a window.

casement window: A window that opens on hinges.

casing: Framework around a door or window.

catch basin: A sievelike device at a sewer's entrance to prevent solid matter from blocking the system.

caulk: To fill seams and joints with a flexible, durable substance to make them watertight and airtight.

cavity wall: Two walls, usually brick, constructed with a hollow space between in which the air serves as insulation. This type of construction also prevents windswept rain from seeping through the interior wall. Ties of metal or brick join the walls. Often called hollow wall.

checking: Cracks that appear in wood which is unevenly seasoned; also fissures on exterior painted surfaces that result from age.

center to center: In measuring spaces between structural members, such as joists and studs, actual distance is from the center of each unit.

cinder block: A building block made of portland cement and crushed cinders.

circuit: Two or more wires through which electricity circulates from the supply source to one or more outlets and then back to the source.

circuit breaker: An advanced safety device that disconnects electrical flow whenever a circuit is overloaded.

clapboard: A long tapered board used as siding for frame dwellings.

common brick: The least expensive red brick used for construction and lacking the attractive texture and water-resistant qualities of tapestry or face brick.

component construction: A method of building in which all units of a house are completely fabricated at the factory and assembled on a site.

concrete block: A rectangular, partially hollow masonry block made of portland cement, sand, and aggregate which is considerably stronger than cinder block and is used in constructing foundations and building walls.

condensation: Droplets of water sometimes appearing as frost on inside surfaces of exterior walls or windows in cold weather, and caused by excessive moisture-laden air in poorly ventilated buildings.

conductors: A widely used trade term for electrical wires.

conduit: 1. A metal tube which covers and protects electric wires. 2. A natural or man-made trough or culvert for carrying water.

crawl space: In basementless houses, a shallow area between floor and ground.

damper: A metal device to regulate draft in the flue of a boiler, furnace, or fireplace.

dead load: An inert weight that remains constant, such as the downward pressure of structural members. *See* live load.

dew point: The temperature at which water vapor in the air begins to condense into droplets.

dormer: A window that projects from a sloping roof.

double-hung window: A window that opens and closes by raising and lowering.

downspout: *See* leader.

dressed lumber: Wood after it has been seasoned and planed. A 2″ x 4″ board when dressed is actually 1⅝″ x 3⅝″.

drip cap: A U-shaped molding installed along the top of a window or door to deflect water beyond the opening.

dry rot: A gradual disintegration of seasoned wood, caused by decay fungi having access to moisture.

dry-wall: A substitute for plaster, which may be gypsum board, plywood, or similar prepared panels.

dry well: A gravel or stone-filled hole in the soil to collect rain runoff from the roof.

ducts: Metal pipes, usually rectangular, which carry forced warm air from the furnace to various parts of the house; also used to circulate cooled air from a conditioning unit.

electric service panel: The main cabinet where electric current enters the house then branches off to different circuits. The main switch to disconnect the entire house current is installed there; also the circuit breakers or fuses.

ell: An addition to a structure at a right angle to its length.

expansion joint: A bituminous fiber placed between separate slabs of concrete, as on a sidewalk, to prevent cracks when rising temperature causes expansion.

facebrick: A type of brick made of selected clays and often textured which is highly water-resistant. Also called tapestry brick.

fiberboard: Insulating material formed into sheets from the pulp fiber of vegetables, wood, or cane.

firebrick: A brick made of special fire clay to resist high heat.

fire clay: Material that can withstand very high temperatures without softening or fusing, and used to line chimney flues and fire chambers of boilers and furnaces.

firestop: Any solid object used to block airways between walls to prevent smoke and fire from spreading.

flagstone: A type of rock that splits readily into layers or flags which is used to pave patios and entrance halls.

flashing: Sheet metal or other material used around chimneys, dormers, windows, and joints where angles meet, to protect a structure from water seepage.

flue: An enclosed chimney passage through which gas and smoke rise to open air.

flue lining: Round or square fire clay or terra-cotta pipe made in two-foot lengths, which prevents smoke and hot gases from escaping through the wall of the chimney into the house. Flue lining should extend from the concrete footing to the top of the chimney cap.

footing: The concrete base or bottom of a foundation, column, or chimney.

frost line: The lowest level at which earth freezes; the depth varies in different latitudes.

furring: Wood strips fastened to a wall, ceiling, or floor to provide an airspace which also serves as a base for lath or dry-wall.

gable: Triangular peaks at either end of the house above the eaves. A ridged roof ending abruptly at both ends is called a gable roof.

girder: A main beam that supports the superstructure.

grade: The slope or pitch of the ground around a house.

grading: Arranging soil to slope downward from a foundation for drainage.

grounding: Linking the electrical system to the earth, a safety measure to prevent damage or fire by lightning, and to avert the hazard of shocks.

grout: Mortar liquefied by adding a large amount of water which is poured into narrow masonry joints and seams.

gutter: A trough or open channel installed below and along roof eaves to carry off rainwater.

half story: An attic in a dwelling with a pitched roof which has a finished ceiling and floor but a low side wall.

half-timbered: An exposed wooden framework, the spaces of which are filled with cement or bricks, as in Tudor architecture.

hardboard: An inexpensive substitute for wood made of finely ground wood fibers bonded under pressure with an adhesive.

hardwood: Lumber from trees that shed their broad leaves in the fall. The term hardwood or softwood is not an accurate index of relative hardness. Some softwoods such as southern yellow pine or Douglas fir are much harder than the hardwoods poplar or basswood. *See* softwood.

hearth: The floor of a fireplace, including the part that extends into the room, constructed of tile, brick, or stone.

hollow tile: Building blocks made of hard clay, used in erecting load-bearing walls, usually faced with brick or stucco.

hollow wall: *See* cavity wall.

hopper window: A window that opens inward on hinges attached to the bottom.

hot wires: Electric lines that conduct power. These are colored black in a 120 volt system, and black and red in a 240 volt system; white wires are neutral.

I-beam: A steel girder having a cross section that resembles the letter I.

insulation: Any substance which is a poor conductor of heat, electricity, or sound and also used as a fire-retardant.

jamb: The upright piece forming the side of an opening, as of a door, window or fireplace.

joists: Planks two to four inches thick and six or more inches wide, which rest on load-bearing walls and beams; used to support floors and ceilings.

kiln-dried: A method of seasoning lumber in ovens, which is a faster process than air-drying.

lally column: A cylindrical hollow steel column usually filled with concrete for added strength and used to support beams.

lath: Wooden strips, metal mesh, gypsum, or insulating board secured to the frame of a structure to serve as a plaster base.

leader: A metal pipe, extending from the roof gutter to the ground, to carry off rainwater. Also called a downspout.

lintel: A length of steel, stone, or wood laid horizontally across the top of a door, window, and other openings, to support the load directly above.

live-load: 1. The shifting weight in a building as its occupants walk about. 2. The weight of furniture and other movable objects in contrast to the dead load of structural members.

load-bearing: Refers to walls that bear weight in addition to their own.

louver: An opening with horizontal slats to ventilate attics and other areas. It is designed to prevent rain or sunlight from entering.

masonry: Anything built of materials, such as concrete, stone, brick, or tile.

millwork: Woodwork that has been finished and partly assembled at the mill.

moisture barrier: A waterproof material placed against the inner side of exterior walls to prevent moisture from forming on the wood. A vapor barrier.

molding: Wood strips machined in various shapes, sizes, and designs for use as ornamental trim.

mortar: A mixture of cement, sand, and water used to bond bricks and stone.

mullion: The thin vertical bar separating window panes.

newel: 1. An upright post that supports the handrail at the top and bottom of a stairway. 2. Any post around which the steps of a winding staircase turn.

party wall: A common wall between two attached houses that is shared and used by each owner.

percolation test: A soil test to ascertain whether water seepage is adequate for a septic tank or cesspool.

pier: A masonry pillar used to support other structural members.

pitch: The incline of a roof from the plate or base to the ridge or peak.

plaster board: Rigid wallboard made of gypsum covered with heavy paper on both sides.

plate: A horizontal length of lumber resting on studs or posts to support rafters.

platform frame: Construction in which floors are framed separately. Each floor is supported by studs that are only one story high.

plywood: Construction material made of three or more layers of thin veneers or sheets of wood glued together with the grain of each sheet at right angles to the other, and manufactured in 3, 5, or 7, ply sheets that do not warp.

prefabricated house: A house in which all units are fabricated in a factory and then shipped to a site for assembling.

quarter round: A molding with a quarter circle profile.

rafter: One of a series of sloping planks designed to support roof loads. Rafters of a flat roof are called joists.

reflective insulation: Aluminum foil-covered insulating material, the effectiveness of which is measured by the number of reflective surfaces rather than thickness.

register: In warm-air heating, a grille that allows the heated air to pass into different rooms.

ridge: The highest line formed by the two sloping surfaces of a roof. Rafters on both inclines are nailed at the ridge.

ridge board: A plank extending the length of the ridge to secure the upper ends of the rafters.

sash: The framing which holds one or more window panes.

semi-detached: A dwelling which shares a common wall with one other house.

sewer trap: A device in the sewer line to prevent sewer gas from seeping into the house without interrupting the flow of sewage.

shake: A handsplit edge-grained shingle, usually of cedar.

sheathing: Wallboard, plywoood, or similar material nailed to exterior studs or rafters which forms the base for finish applications.

shingles: Small rectangular or square pieces of building material laid in overlapping rows on the roof or walls of a house.

short circuit: A faulty connection that causes the circuit breaker or fuse to break the flow of electricity in the circuit.

siding: The finish or outer covering of a frame house, such as wood, shingle, aluminum, vinyl, stucco, or other protective material.

sill: The lowest wooden member of a building, resting horizontally on the foundation and providing the support or bearing surface for the beam, joists, and exterior walls of the structure.

slate: Natural stone that splits easily into flat sheets of varying thickness which provides a durable, finished roofing material and also is used for patios.

soffit: The underside of parts of a building, such as a stairway, arch, cornice, or beam.

softwood: Cone-bearing, evergreen trees which, except for the cypress and larch, do not shed their needle-like leaves. *See* hardwood.

soil stack: The main vertical pipe in the plumbing system which receives all waste matter from other units.

sole plate: A horizontal board, usually 2″ x 4″, on which the wall studs rest.

solid brick construction: A type of house construction with brick walls built several courses thick to support the weight of the entire structure.

structural lighting: Lighting devised to fit a specific purpose.

stucco: An exterior finish usually consisting of portland cement, lime, and sand.

stud: A vertical length of lumber, 2″ x 4″, used to form the framework of a wall or partition, the length of which determines the height of the ceiling. In the plural, often called studding.

subfloor: In better-built houses, a rough flooring laid directly on the joists that provides a rigid base for the finish flooring.

sump pump: An apparatus to siphon water from basements, particularly those below sewer level, that cannot be waterproofed and are subject to seepage or floods.

termite shield: A flat strip of noncorrosive metal placed between the foundation and superstructure, and around pipes that extend through the foundation, to prevent termite infestation.

terra-cotta: A glazed or unglazed baked clay used in the building industry for roofing, facing, and ornamental work.

terrazzo: Flooring of small different colored marble chips embedded in cement and polished.

three-way switch: A switch controlling lighting in a room at both ends or in a stairway at upper and lower levels. A switch is installed at each location.

trim: Interior finishing materials, such as moldings, usually ornamental, applied to doors, windows, baseboards, cornices, and other objects.

valley: An internal or depressed angle formed by the junction at the bottom of two sloping sides of the roof.

vapor barrier: *See* moisture barrier.

vitrified tile: Pipes formed of very hard baked clay, often glazed, frequently used for underground drainage.

wainscot: Wood paneling or other material on the lower half of walls.

wallboard: A fabricated, rigid sheet made of gypsum, compressed wood, or similar materials used to cover walls or ceilings.

water table: A ledge or slight shoulder, usually above a foundation wall, that diverts rain water away from the wall.

weephole: A small opening in the lower part of a retaining wall to allow drainage of excess water.

Glossary: Legal Terms

abstract of title: A compact summary of all recorded documents dealing with title to property and arranged in the order the documents were recorded.

accrued interest: Interest which has been earned, but is not due and payable.

acre: A unit of land amounting to 43,560 square feet or 4,840 square yards.

adjacent: Nearby but not necessarily in physical contact.

adjoining: In actual contact; attached or contiguous.

adverse possession: The acquisition of title to property by actual, open, exclusive, and continuous occupancy of the land for the required statutory duration. Duration varies according to state laws.

affidavit: A declaration in writing sworn to or affirmed before a notary public or other officer authorized to administer an oath or affirmation.

agency: A relationship between principal and agent, such as seller and broker, that arises from a contract, written or oral, employing the agent to sell property.

agreement of sale: A written agreement between a seller and buyer concerning real estate in which both concur to the conditions and terms of the contract. Also called a contract of sale.

amenities: The pleasant surroundings and environment, either natural or created, that contribute to the value and attractiveness of real property.

amortization: Repayment of a loan in regular installments.

apportionments: Adjustment of all expenses or carrying charges and income (if any) calculated to the date of the closing, when the deed is given to the buyer. All expenses to that date are paid by the seller. From then on all expenses are borne by the buyer.

appraisal: An estimate of the current market value of property by a qualified appraiser.

appraisal by comparison: An estimate of property value by comparing sales prices of similar, nearby properties.

appraised value: A value lower than a home's actual worth on the market set by the lender's appraiser. To further protect the lender's investment, loans are given at appraised rather than market values. Thus a $30,000 house may be appraised at only $25,000 for a 70 percent mortgage ($17,500), which can be recovered readily in case the borrower defaults.

appurtenance: Property rights, such as a right-of-way or easement, legally a part of a parcel of land transferred with the title.

assessed valuation: A valuation placed upon property by an employee for the village, town, or city, as a basis for taxation.

assessment: A special charge levied against real estate by a local government unit to cover a proportionate cost of an improvement, such as a sewer or a paved street.

assignment: The transfer of property or a right to another person.

assumption of mortgage: The acceptance of title to property by a person who assumes responsibility to pay the existing mortgage, and who becomes personally liable for the payment of this debt.

attest: To witness by observation and signature.

bill of lading: An agreement between shipper (customer) and carrier (mover); an itemized list of services that is prepared when the shipment is packed and loaded on the van.

bill of sale: A written document which transfers title to personal property from seller to buyer.

binder: A deposit by a buyer of real estate as evidence of good faith; also the written agreement binding the parties.

blanket mortgage: A single mortgage that includes two or more parcels of real estate.

bona fide: In good faith; without intent to defraud.

bond: A written agreement in which the borrower promises to repay the mortgage loan to the lender, and specifying the principal, interest, and terms of payment toward liquidating the debt.

building codes: Regulations devised by local governments specifying, in detail, structural requirements for buildings.

building line: A line fixed at a given distance from the front and/or sides of a lot, beyond which no structure may protrude.

building loan agreement: A contract specifying the amount of money advanced to an owner, and payments to be made at varying stages of construction.

certificate of completion: A voucher for payment signed by the home owner, affirming that he is satisfied with the work and materials and authorizes the lender to pay the contractor. This is a protective measure under FHA improvement loans.

certificate of deposit: A document issued by a bank showing that a given sum of money has been deposited, and payable to certain persons or to the bearer of the certificate.

certificate of occupancy: A document issued by the local government's Buildings Department denoting compliance with all pertinent regulations.

certified check: A negotiable instrument issued by a bank certifying that cash in the amount listed will be paid to the bearer on demand. Unlike personal checks, those certified are the bank's guarantee of payment. Certified checks are commonly used in real estate transactions.

chain of title: The history of ownership of property dating back to the time the original deed was granted, or as far back as records are available.

chattel: Personal property such as household goods or fixtures.

chattel mortgage: A mortgage on personal property.

closing: The actual transfer of property from seller to buyer at which time all final documents are executed; mortgage funds are passed from lender to borrower to seller; a property deed and other evidence of title are given by the seller to the buyer. Lawyers for both principals usually guide these arrangements.

closing costs: All expenses paid by the buyer before he receives the deed; also called settlement costs.

cloud on the title: A substantial claim or encumbrance that impairs the owner's title to property.

condemnation: The acquisition of private property for public use, such as a highway, with reasonable compensation to the owner.

conditional sales contract: An agreement to sell property, with the seller retaining title until all contractual obligations have been fulfilled.

consignee: The person who accepts a shipment at its destination.

conveyance: A written document that transfers ownership of real estate from one party to another.

covenants: Binding agreements written into deeds by former owners to do, or not to do, specific things. If the covenants are not in violation of public policy, they are binding against all subsequent owners and are enforceable by court action.

deed: A written document, containing a detailed description of the property, given by the seller to the buyer at the closing when ownership is actually transferred.

deed of trust: A substitute for a mortgage used in some states.

deed restriction: A restriction imposed in a deed to limit the use of property against certain uses, such as a liquor store, or the size and type of improvements.

deficiency judgment: A judgment against the borrower for the unpaid difference when property in a foreclosure sale sells for less than the amount owed to the mortgage lender.

descent: Real property inherited by the closest relative of those who died leaving no will or an invalid one.

description: A representation by words to identify a parcel of real estate, so its boundaries can be readily recognized. Based on a survey, the description may be a lot or block number or natural or man-made markers.

easement: The right that the public or an individual may have on, over, or through the land of others.

eminent domain: The right of a government to take private property for public use by condemnation.

encroachment: A structure or obstruction that intrudes upon the property of another.

encumbrance: A claim or lien on property that reduces its value.

equity: The amount of value in property the owner has over and above liens against it. As mortgage payments are made, the owner's equity in his property increases.

equity of redemption: The right of an owner to reclaim his property before it is sold through foreclosure. This proceeding can be stopped by paying the debt, interest, and costs.

escrow: A written agreement providing that certain documents or property be put in care of a third party until specified conditions are fulfilled.

estoppel certificate: A document given by the mortgage lender, sometimes by the seller, to the buyer listing the amounts paid and still owed on the mortgage. If a buyer, relying on this statement, discovers the amount is false, the signer of the estoppel certificate must bear the full loss. He would be "estopped" from successfully denying it.

exclusive agency: An agreement between seller and broker for a certain period. If a sale is effected by any other broker, the broker holding the exclusive agency is entitled to full compensation, as is the broker who made the sale. But if the owner himself sells his property, the broker is *not* entitled to any commission.

exclusive right to sell: An agreement similar to exclusive agency except that if the owner himself makes the sale, the broker holding the exclusive right to sell agency is legally entitled to a full commission.

extension agreement: An agreement that extends the life of a mortgage to a later date.

Federal Housing Administration (FHA): A Federal agency established by Congress in 1934, to prevent a recurrence of countless foreclosures resulting from unsound mortgage practices. The FHA insures mortgages to promote sound financing methods. Loans insured by this agency are made by private FHA-approved lenders. FHA itself does not lend money or construct dwellings In 1965 the FHA was made part of the Department of Housing and Urban Development (HUD).

fixtures: Personal property so attached to the land or dwelling that it becomes part of the real property.

foreclosure: A proceeding in which property is sold to pay a debt on which the borrower defaulted.

front foot: A method of measuring property for sale or valuation purposes in which each running foot measured along the street line extends the full depth of the lot.

GI loan: *See* Veterans Administration.

good and marketable title: A title free from any encumbrance or cloud. Contracts often contain this clause.

institutional lenders: Banks, life insurance companies, and savings and loan associations; also called lending institutions.

instrument: A formal legal document, such as a contract or deed.

insurable title: A title to real property that is free of any serious defect and on which a title insurance company will grant an insurance policy.

involuntary lien: A lien, for unpaid taxes or special assessments, imposed against real estate without the owner's consent.

judgment: A court decision awarding a creditor a sum of money against a debtor, which is filed with the county clerk and becomes a lien on all the debtor's property in the county.

junior mortgage: A mortgage that is subordinate to a first mortgage; a second or third mortgage.

lien: A legal claim against another's property for unpaid debts, as a mechanic's lien. Other liens are a mortgage and judgment.

listing: An oral or written agreement between seller and broker to sell or lease real estate.

market value: The highest price at which real estate can sell in an open market, and which is acceptable to the seller free of any pressure to divest himself of the property.

mechanic's lien: A claim created by law and valid in most states which assures the payment for labor and materials used in construction. The debt is recoverable by filing a proper notice or lien with the county clerk within a prescribed period.

metes (measures) and bounds (directions): Description in a deed defining natural or artificial boundary marks or lines.

mill: One-tenth of one cent, the monetary unit on which the tax rate of property is based. Thus a tax rate of one mill per dollar is equal to the rate of one-tenth of one percent of the property's assessed value.

mortgage: A written document in which the borrower's property is pledged as security for the loan. The mortgage creates a legal claim on the property until the debt is paid in full.

mortgage commitment: A formal written communication by the lending institution that it will grant a mortgage loan on property, specifying the amount, as well as length of time.

mortgagee: The lender or lending institution.

mortgagor: One who borrows money and gives a mortgage on his property.

multiple listing: An arrangement among brokers in a given locality by which each broker pools his listings with the others. If a sale follows, the commission is divided between the broker who furnished the listing and the broker making the sale.

net listing: The minimum selling price set by a property owner. The broker effecting the sale receives the amount over and above the net listing as his commission.

notary public: A public officer authorized to attest deeds and other documents to make them authentic and to take affidavits.

open-end mortgage: A provision allowing the property owner to borrow additional money at a future date. The amount usually does not exceed the sum already paid on the original loan.

open listing: A listing open to any broker, with the commission due only to the agent who first finds a buyer ready, willing, and able to meet the seller's terms.

option: A written agreement between a property owner and another person in which the latter has the right to buy the property at a fixed price within a specified period of time.

police power: **1.** The inherent right of a government—local, state, or federal—to initiate measures for public health, safety, and general welfare. **2.** In real estate, the right to acquire land for public use.

prepayment clause: A clause permitting the borrower to pay his mortgage in part or in full without penalty before it becomes due.

principal: A person who employs an agent to perform certain acts, such as buying or selling property for him.

prospectus: A printed introductory proposal or offer to sell homes in a new development.

purchase money mortgage: A mortgage held by the seller who accepts part of the purchase price in cash and holds the mortgage as security against payment of the balance.

real property: Land and all structures built on it.

realtor: Coined word for a real estate agent who belongs to the local board, affiliated with the National Association of Real Estate Boards.

redemption: The right of a home owner to redeem property by paying a debt after a certain date and before the sale at foreclosure; also the right of an owner to reclaim his property before its sale for unpaid taxes.

riparian: Relating to the banks of any waterway, as a stream or river. A riparian owner has land bordering water.

satisfaction piece: A formal paper given by the lender to the borrower upon full payment of the mortgage loan to acknowledge liquidation of the debt.

seal: Initially an impression in a molten wafer of wax made with a signet device, containing a crest or coat of arms, on a document to signify its authenticity, now replaced by the letters "L.S."—*locus sigilli*—(the place of the seal), for the signature.

separate property: Property individually owned by either wife or husband and obtained by either spouse before marriage, or by gift or inheritance after marriage.

seller's lien: A claim which a seller holds upon his materials until he is paid in full.

setback: The distance measured from the curb for a prescribed depth into the property on which no structure may be built.

settlement costs: *See* closing costs.

severalty ownership: Real estate owned by only one person.

solvency: The ability to pay debts, as mortgage payments, when they are due.

specific performance: A court decree to compel a defaulting party to carry out the terms of a contract.

straight mortgage: A type of mortgage seldom used today, but common before the great depression of 1929, in which payments were only on interest, and the full principal became due at maturity; also known as a fixed mortgage.

statute of frauds: A law that requires all real estate agreements and certain other contracts on real property to be in writing. Oral contracts on real property are not enforceable in court.

tare weight: The weight of goods minus the weight of moving van.

tax deed: A deed given to the buyer of real estate sold or auctioned publicly by a local government for non-payment of taxes.

title insurance: An insurance policy to indemnify the holder against any loss of property sustained by defects in the title.

title search: An examination of all recorded documents relating to past ownership of real property.

unearned increment: A rise in real estate value through no effort by the owner, usually following population growth and inflation.

usury: Interest rates exceeding those permitted by state law. Penalties for this practice vary from loss of interest to full loss of principal.

variable rate: An escalation clause in the mortgage loan contract allowing the lender to increase interest rates to equal those of the common market—an alleged advantage to the borrower for decreased interest rates if the rates decline in the open market.

Veterans Administration: A government agency which, under the Servicement's Readjustment Act of 1944, guarantees VA loans. To encourage private lending agencies to give longer mortgages to veterans, the VA guarantees up to 60 percent of the amount. Granted for terms up to 30 years, VA loans are restricted to honorably discharged veterans and their widows only.

zoning: The right of a municipality to regulate and determine the compatible character and use of property.

INDEX

Acoustical materials, 74
Air-conditioning, 116–119
  zone map for, 116–117
A-line house, 151
Alterations. *See* Home improvement
American Society for Testing Materials, 112
American Standards Association, 112
Appliances, 86, 87, 197
  allowance for replacement of, 230
  FHA loans for, 202
  included in contract of sale, 180
  wattage table, 94
Appraisal
  for buyer, 27
  for condemnation, 207
  for easement, 208
  by FHA, 162–164
Appraised value, 166, 170, 175
Architect, 24, 29–31, 49
Assessed valuation, 12, 13, 22, 198
Assessments, 22, 26, 198
  liability of seller for, 199
  for sanitation services, 15, 104
  special, 176, 198, 199
  tax lien for, 206
Attached house, 45–46, 63
Attic, 4, 58, 108
Attorney Reference Service, 159

Banks, 157, 184
  building and loan associations, 162
  commercial, 168, 204

cooperative banks, 167
mutual savings bank, 168
savings and loan associations, 160, 167
Bar Association, 159
Basement, 54–55
  inspection of, 64–65, 68, 85
Basementless house, 55, 64
Bathrooms, 28, 53–54
Beach house, 151, 153
Beam, 68
Belcher, Donald, 7
Better Business Bureau, 139, 141, 174, 175, 187
Bi-level house, 33, 36–39
Bill of sale, 180
Binder, 158, 178
  protective clause in, 178
Boilers, 110–115, 201
Bond (note), 160
  labor and material, 141
  performance, 141
Brick
  types of, 71
  veneer, 70, 71, 72
Bridging, 78, 79
British thermal unit (Btu) table, 119
Broker. *See* Mortgage broker; Real estate brokers
Buffer strip, 17
Builder. *See* Contractor
Building codes, 19, 24–25, 62
  Inspection Service, 139

249

NOTES